# Open for Debate

# The Arab-Israeli
# Conflict

Open for Debate

# The Arab-Israeli
# Conflict

## Richard Worth

**Marshall Cavendish**
Benchmark
New York

With thanks to Ilham Nasser, visiting researcher at the Center for Global Peace at American University, in Washington, D.C., for her expert review of this manuscript.

Marshall Cavendish Benchmark
99 White Plains Road
Tarrytown, NY 10591-9001
www.marshallcavendish.us

Library of Congress Cataloging-in-Publication Data
Worth, Richard.
The Arab-Israeli conflict / by Richard Worth.
p. cm. — (Open for debate)
Summary: "Outlines the history, origins, and different perspectives of the Arab-Israeli conflict"—Provided by publisher. Includes bibliographical references and index.
ISBN-13: 978-0-7614-2295-2
ISBN-10: 0-7614-2295-1
1. Arab-Israeli conflict—1993—Juvenile literature. I. Title.
II. Series.
DS119.76.W67 2006
956.9405—dc22
2005029049

Photo research by Linda Sykes, Hilton Head, SC

Reuters/Corbis: cover and pages 1, 2–3, 5; Suhaib Salem/Reuters/Corbis: 6;
Avi Ohayon/Government Press Office/ Handout/Reuters/Corbis: 9; Ammar Awad/
Reuters/Corbis: 19; Gianni Dagli Orti/Corbis: 21; Hulton-Deutsch Collection/Corbis: 37;
Bettmann-Corbis: 39, 53, 71; Hulton-Deutsch Collection/Corbis: 47; Tim Page/Corbis: 54;
Owen Franken/Corbis: 57; David Rubinger/Corbis: 83; Reuters/Corbis: 88, 105;
Peter Turnley/Corbis: 93; Ed Kashi/Corbis: 103.

Editorial Director: Michelle Bisson
Art Director: Anahid Hamparian
Series Designer: Sonia Chaghatzbanian

Printed in China
1 3 5 6 4 2

# Contents

A **Palestinian** boy places a **Palestinian** flag on top of a destroyed house during celebrations of the impending pull-out from **Gaza** by the **Israeli** government.

# Portrait of a Tragic Conflict

On September 12, 2005, the last Israeli flag was taken down in the Gaza Strip, a narrow ribbon of land located along the Mediterranean Sea in the Middle East. Israel had occupied this territory for almost four decades, following the Six Day War in 1967. Israelis regarded the Gaza Strip as part of their historic homeland. Palestinians, on the other hand, believed that the Gaza Strip should form the nucleus of a new Palestinian state.

As the Israeli flag came down, it was soon replaced by Palestinian flags. As one Palestinian leader, Daman Hajaj, put it, "as long as we feel freedom, I feel wonderful, and I feel freedom today."

Since the end of the Six Day War, Israelis had gradually established settlements in the Gaza Strip. By 2005, approximately ten thousand Israelis lived there in twenty-five settlements. Gaza was also home to more than one million Palestinians, who regarded the presence of Israeli settlers as a threat to a future Palestinian state. In 2004, Israeli Prime Minister Ariel Sharon announced that the Israeli settlements in Gaza would be dismantled by his government. This was a major turnaround for Sharon. For many years, Sharon had been a major supporter of building more Israeli settlements.

Nevertheless, Sharon realized that Israeli withdrawal from Gaza might be necessary to future relations between Israel and the Palestinians. In addition, longtime Palestinian leader Yasir Arafat died late in 2004. He was replaced by Mahmoud Abbas, who seemed more willing to talk peace. Before Arafat's death, both sides had been locked in a brutal struggle since 2000, called the Intifada. This was an uprising of Palestinians who lived in the Gaza Strip and in settlements along the West Bank of the Jordan River. Arab youths clashed with the Israeli Defense Force (IDF) in Gaza and the West Bank. Meanwhile, young Palestinian suicide bombers went into Israel where they blew themselves up and took the lives of innocent Israeli citizens, some of them children. Sharon's announcement that Israel would evacuate its settlements in Gaza helped bring an end to the Intifada.

While a majority of Israelis supported the withdrawal, many settlers in Gaza were opposed to it. All the settlers were supposed to have left their homes by August 15, 2005. But, as of that date, about five thousand remained. The Israeli military was, therefore, forced to enter the settlements and forcibly remove the remaining settlers. Some settlers tried to barricade the gates to their communities to keep out the military. Others barricaded themselves inside their homes. Still others retreated to rooftops and sprayed the soldiers with acid.

However, the Israeli military succeeded in removing the resisters. As reporter Steven Erlanger of the *New York Times* wrote, "The mood was somber and serious with experienced soldiers and police officers quietly trying to negotiate voluntary departures first with sometimes hysterical settlers. . . . Only later were the crowbars unpacked and doors forced open . . . in some cases [soldiers were] dragging parents away in front of their frightened

ON FEBRUARY 20, 2005, ISRAELI PRIME MINISTER ARIEL SHARON SIGNED EVACUATION ORDERS FOR THE SETTLEMENTS IN THE GAZA STRIP. THE ISRAELI GOVERNMENT HAD NEVER BEFORE DECIDED TO DISMANTLE SETTLEMENTS ON LANDS PALESTINIANS WANTED FOR THEIR INDEPENDENT STATE.

children. . . " In addition to the settlements in Gaza, the Israeli government also gave up several small settlements on the West Bank.

While the world press was covering the Israeli pullout, the Palestinians felt almost overlooked. One Palestinian living in Gaza spoke for many other residents. As Suheil Abu al-Araj put it, "Maybe I shouldn't mention this. I saw a settler crying on television. But they've been settlers for what, 20 years? What about those who stayed refugees for 50 years? They are victims, and we are victims, too." He was referring to the Palestinians who fled Palestine in 1948 during the civil war between Arabs and Jews that led to the founding of Israel.

Many Palestinians not only want to regain Gaza but land on the West Bank and the city of Jerusalem, which they believe belongs to them. One large sign in Gaza said, "Gaza today, the West Bank and Jerusalem tomorrow."

## Elements of the Struggle

The struggle between Arabs and Israelis is a brutal conflict that has been going on for more than half a century. The dimensions of the struggle are often hard to untangle, but they involve several key elements.

- **A military struggle between Israelis and Palestinians for the same land.**
- **The Palestinian right to return to land that they claim as their own.**
- **The intentions of the PLO as the representative of the Palestinian people.**
- **Expanding Jewish settlements on land, called the occupied territories, that is claimed by Palestinians.**
- **The role of the United States in the Middle East.**

- **The struggle between Israeli and Palestinian leaders, such as Yasir Arafat, former head of the PLO, and Ariel Sharon, former prime minister of Israel.**
- **The future of negotiations between Israel and the Palestinians in the post-Arafat, post-Sharon era.**

## The Struggle for Land

The land of Israel is claimed by two different groups. Jews began settling in the area, known as Palestine, during Biblical times, more than three thousand years ago. They established a kingdom, with a capital in Jerusalem. However, the Jews were later driven out of Palestine by the Romans during the first century CE. During the seventh century, the prophet Muhammad founded a new religion, known as Islam. After Muhammad's death, Muslims—followers of Islam—conquered vast areas in the Middle East, including Palestine. Muslims remained in control of Palestine into the nineteenth century, when Jews began returning to the area.

During the twentieth century, a struggle between Jews and Muslims broke out for control of Palestine. The United Nations planned to partition the area into Jewish and Palestinian states. Before this occurred, fighting broke out between Muslims and Jews.

The Arabs rejected partition. They expected to run a Palestinian state where Jews would be subordinate to Arabs. If the Jews did not like this situation, the Arabs were happy to have them leave.

Israelis felt quite differently. According to historian Cheryl Rubenberg, author of *The Palestinians: In Search of a Just Peace*, Israeli leader David Ben-Gurion planned to drive the Arabs out of Palestine. As Ben-Gurion wrote: "We must expel Arabs and take their places . . . and if we

have to use force . . . then we have force at our disposal."
Nevertheless, the Israeli constitution gave Arabs and Israelis equal citizenship.

## Palestinian Right of Return

Jews and Palestinians also disagree over what happened to
the Arabs living in the area that became the state of Israel.
Palestinians admit that some of them left voluntarily to
flee the dangers of war that broke out in 1948. Yet, as
Rubenberg adds, "they departed without their possessions
and did not sell their properties, indicating their expecta-
tions to return." The rest were driven out by the Israeli
army. The Israelis also may have destroyed more than 340
Palestinian villages. Jews counter that many Palestinians
left voluntarily because they planned to return after the defeat of the Jews. As Israel proclaimed independence, the
nation was invaded by surrounding Arab states—Jordan,
Egypt, and Syria. But the IDF defeated the Arab armies. As
a result, the Palestinians never returned.

The right of return has become a central issue in the
Arab-Israeli conflict. Palestinians believe that they should
be allowed to come back to Israel and reclaim their lands.
Israelis counter that Palestinians left of their own accord
and have no right to come back. This conflict grew even
greater in 1967. Jews expanded the state of Israel as a re-
sult of the Six-Day War with surrounding Arab nations.
The war began when Israel launched its air force against
Arab military targets. This occurred after Egypt blockaded
Israeli ports. Israel expanded its territory onto the West
Bank of the Jordan River and the Gaza Strip, the home of
many Palestinian refugees since 1948, and ruled by Egypt.
In addition, the Israeli government took over control of
Jerusalem, which they claim as their ancient capital. Pales-
tinians, and other Muslims, believe that Jerusalem was the
site where the prophet Muhammad ascended into heaven.

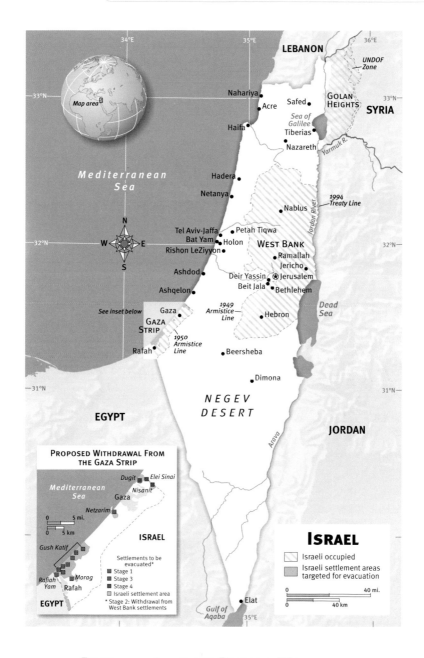

**PRESENT-DAY ISRAEL AND PROPOSED WITHDRAWAL
FROM GAZA STRIP**

(Christians consider the city sacred as the place where Jesus Christ was crucified.) Palestinians have also claimed that the West Bank is their territory. Jews call the West Bank Judea and Samaria, and claim it as part of the ancient Jewish homeland. Israelis say that life has improved for Palestinians since the West Bank became part of Israel. Many Palestinians have gone to work in Israel. Approximately two thousand industrial plants were set up by Israel in the newly occupied lands. Indeed, the West Bank was among the fastest growing economic areas of the world during the last part of the twentieth century. Perhaps because they were receiving Israeli health services Palestinian life expectancy had risen to seventy-two by the start of the twenty-first century from only forty-eight in 1967. Palestinians point out that since the Intifada broke out in 2000, all these benefits have ended. Indeed, most Palestinians are now prevented from working in Israel, and Palestinian unemployment has skyrocketed, reaching 75 percent in parts of Gaza. Palestinians also emphasize that Israel intends to continue occupying the West Bank that Arabs call their own. As Israel's former Attorney General Michael Ben-Yair stated in 2002, "We enthusiastically chose to become a colonial society, ignoring international treaties, expropriating lands, transferring settlers from Israel to the occupied territories . . . and finding justification for all these activities . . ." Indeed, more than 50 percent of the land on the West Bank and Gaza has been turned over to Jewish settlers.

## The Intentions of the PLO and Yasir Arafat

The leading spokesman for the Palestinians opposing the Israeli occupation was, until his death late in 2004, Yasir Arafat. In 1964, Arafat founded the Palestinian Liberation Organization (PLO). The PLO's charter called for the destruction of the state of Israel, primarily through violence; the return of the Palestinians to their homeland; and the establishment of a Palestinian state. The Palestinians claimed that they were subjected to violence by the Israelis in the West Bank and Gaza. According to the human rights group Amnesty International, the Israelis have used torture against Palestinian prisoners. The IDF also destroyed thousands of homes owned by the families of people who have been arrested and charged with terrorist activities. Israeli prime ministers have not hesitated to launch attacks against PLO leaders, sometimes killing innocent civilians.

Meanwhile, Arafat and the PLO launched terrorist attacks on Israel from bases in Jordan and later from occupied areas of Lebanon during the 1970s and 1980s. But when violence did not bring the Palestinians a homeland, Arafat publicly stated in the late 1980s that the PLO had renounced violence. As a result, peace negotiations followed between the PLO and Israel, leading to a Palestinian territory in Gaza and part of the West Bank in the 1990s. This was governed by the Palestinian Authority, led by Yasir Arafat.

But many people wondered whether Arafat had really changed. Had he really renounced violence? Terrorist acts continued during the negotiations with the Israelis that led to a Palestinian territory. Even after the Palestinian Authority had been established, with Arafat in charge, terrorism continued. Arafat claimed that radical groups were acting without his consent. But Jewish authors Barry and Judith Rubin disagree. There was "much evidence that Arafat was tolerating . . . terrorist groups, making him seem unworthy of trust and likely to take advantage of Israeli concessions to create a more dangerous situation." Indeed, it seems likely that he never gave up the idea of destroying Israel.

Israel retaliated by killing some of the radical Palestinian leaders. Many Israelis believed that since Arafat could not be trusted to live in peace with Jews, the only solution was

15

violence. The level of violence increased during the 1990s. Finally, in 2000 the Israeli government offered Arafat a deal. He would be able to establish a new Palestinian state in Gaza and much of the West Bank, with its capital in East Jerusalem.

## The Settlement Issue

Arafat turned down the deal. Was he simply being inflexible? Many Jewish observers believed that this was the only explanation for his decision. But Faisal Husseini, who was involved in the negotiations in 2000, disagreed. The Rubins cite Husseini as saying, "Israel wants to determine the permanent borders based on the settlements. We say the fate of the settlements will be determined by the borders." In other words, according to Husseini, Israel must be willing to withdraw to its borders before the 1967 war. This means all settlements on the West Bank and in Gaza must be removed.

Since 1967, approximately eight thousand Israeli settlers have established homes in the Gaza Strip. Many thousands more have moved onto the West Bank. Israelis claim that they have a right to occupy this land. They also regard the settlements as a barrier against an attack against central Israel by the Arabs. Palestinians believe the settlements mean that Israel will never return this land to the Palestinian Authority so that it can become part of a new Palestinian state.

## Role of the United States

From the founding of Israel in 1948, the United States has been its strongest ally. Americans felt that Jews were owed a huge debt after six million of them were killed by Nazis in Europe during the Holocaust. In addition, Jews in the United States form a powerful, well-financed lobbying group on behalf of Israel. U.S. political leaders are often reluctant to oppose Israeli interests and lose the votes of American Jews. Nevertheless, several American presidents have tried to broker peace between Israel and the Arab nations. During the 1970s, President Jimmy Carter helped secure a peace agreement between Israel and Egypt. As part of the deal, the United States supplied millions of dollars in aid to both nations. During the 1980s, the American government also helped Israel and the PLO make a peace agreement. This led to the establishment of a Palestinian government in the Gaza Strip.

However, Arab leaders have often criticized the United States for using different criteria for judging Israel and the other nations of the Middle East. After the 1967 war, Israel occupied Palestinian territory on the West Bank. The United States did not force the Israelis to withdraw. In contrast, some Arab leaders pointed out that the United States formed a coalition to oust Saddam Hussein from Kuwait after his invasion of the country in 1990. President Bill Clinton blamed PLO leader Yasir Arafat for not making a deal with the Israelis in 2000. Arabs say that deal would have required the PLO to give up any hope of regaining control of sacred Muslim religious shrines in Jerusalem and would have left Palestinian areas fragmented and without free access to one another. More recently President George W. Bush refused to deal with Arafat. He criticized him for not wanting peace and called for his replacement. Bush made clear that the United States strongly supported Israeli leader Ariel Sharon. Meanwhile, Sharon refused to deal with Arafat. By 2006, this issue was moot, as Arafat had died and Sharon was in a coma. Two new governments would have to deal with each other.

## Israeli and Palestinian Leaders

For many years, Israeli and Palestinian leaders were locked in conflict. One of these leaders was Yasir Arafat. Another leader who long played an important role in the conflict was former Israeli Prime Minister Ariel Sharon. A former army general, Sharon helped win the 1967 war and later in the 1980s drove the PLO out of Lebanon. Sharon championed a hard line in Israel's dealings with the PLO, believing that violence should be met with violence. He was also a champion of building new settlements. After serving as defense minister and housing minister—in charge of settlements—Sharon finally became Israeli prime minister in 2001. Meanwhile, an Intifada had broken out on the West Bank and in Gaza. It was met with massive retaliation by the IDF, which took over much of those territories.

Conservative columnist James Kitfield of the *National Journal* wrote, "Ariel Sharon and Yasir Arafat increasingly seemed locked in a death grip at the end of a decades-long grudge match that has largely defined each man's political life." This conflict was also an element in the larger Israeli-Palestinian confrontation.

Sharon himself said that he wanted "to create in the Arabs a psychology of defeat, to beat them every time and to beat them so decisively that they would develop the conviction that they would never win." Yet, early in 2004, Sharon announced that he was ready to withdraw all Israeli settlements from Gaza and hand the area completely over to the Palestinians.

Had Sharon suddenly changed? Journalist Henry Siegman wrote that Sharon was only willing to give up Gaza to retain control of the West Bank.

## The New Leaders

Following the death of Yasir Arafat, elections in 2005 brought a new prime minister to the Palestinian territories—Mahmoud Abbas. Along with Arafat, Abbas had helped found the PLO and had participated in many of the peace talks with the Israelis. Unlike Arafat, however, Abbas

**PALESTINIAN PRESIDENT MAHMOUD ABBAS GREETS PROTESTORS IN THE WEST BANK CALLING FOR THE RELEASE OF PALESTINIANS FROM ISRAELI JAILS.**

committed himself to stopping Palestinian violence by demanding that Palestinians stop terrorist acts. In January 2006, Prime Minister Sharon suffered a massive stroke that removed him from office. He was replaced as prime minister at the end of March by Ehud Olmert, who had been acting prime minister since Sharon's stroke. After Sharon's stroke, also in January, the terrorist group Hamas won control of the Palestinian parliament in national elections. Many Palestinians believed that PLO leaders were guilty of corruption and had mismanaged the government. These major changes left the future of Israeli-Palestinian relations very much in doubt.

# Struggle for Land

At the center of the Arab-Israeli conflict is the same land claimed by both Jews and Muslims. This clash centers on Jerusalem and the present-day nation of Israel. Each side claims the same land. Thus, land is at the heart of the conflict.

## The Land of Israel

Israel is a long, narrow country about the size of the state of New Jersey. In the south is a dry area, known as the Negev Desert. Westward, along the Mediterranean Sea, is a strip of rich, fertile land and seaports. To the north are lush hills and valleys, and eastward is the Sea of Galilee—the ancient center of the Jewish nation.

Approximately 3,500 years ago, an area known as Canaan was inhabited by a variety of tribes, including the Hebrews. Some of the Hebrews had lived in Mesopotamia (present-day Iraq and Syria) while others were subjects of the Egyptian pharaoh, or king. During the thirteenth century BCE, Moses brought the Hebrews out of Egypt to Canaan, a land that they conquered and called Israel.

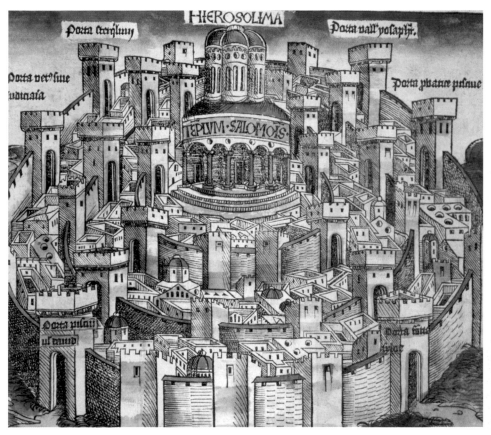

Porta ctrglimy  HIEROSOLIMA  Porta uall' yosaplyr.

Porta uer'sune  Porta phatue psanc

udtaata

TEPLVM·SALOMOIS

Porta pisan  Porta sue

ul onud

**DURING THE MIDDLE AGES, JEWS IN JERUSALEM WERE PERSECUTED BY CHRISTIANS, BUT LIVED IN HARMONY WITH THE MUSLIM POPULATION.**

About 1000 BCE, King David established the capital of Israel in Jerusalem. During the tenth century, David's son Solomon built a magnificent house of worship in Jerusalem. Called the First Temple, it was constructed at a site called the Temple Mount. After Solomon's death, however, the land split into two parts—the north, which continued to be called Israel, and the south, known as Judah, from which the word Jew is taken. Both were controlled by the Jews.

Over the next thousand years, Israel and Judah were conquered and reconquered by foreign rulers who destroyed the Temple. After a brief period of independence lasting about a century, the Jews were defeated by the Romans in 63 BCE. The Romans incorporated the area that they called Judea into their vast empire. Rome established a local leader named Herod as the ruler of the Jews. Herod was known as the Great, because he constructed so many magnificent buildings in Jerusalem, including a larger Temple.

In the last years of Herod's reign, according to the Bible, a baby named Jesus was born in Bethlehem, located in eastern Judea. Jesus founded a new religion, called Christianity. When Jesus was later crucified in Jerusalem, Christians believed that he miraculously returned to life there and later ascended into heaven. As Christianity gradually began to spread across the Roman Empire, Christians regarded Jerusalem as sacred to their faith.

Meanwhile, the Jews had staged revolts against the Romans in 66 CE and again in 132 CE. Both rebellions were crushed by the Roman leaders who destroyed the Temple, drove out the Jews from Jerusalem, and renamed the area Palestine.

## Arrival of the Muslims

Palestine remained part of the Roman Empire for several centuries, but by about 500 CE, Rome had been overrun by Germanic tribes. About 570 CE, a child named Muhammad was born in Mecca, located in the present-day nation of Saudi Arabia. When he was twenty-five, Muhammad went to work in a business owned by a wealthy woman named Khadijah. Although he was fifteen years younger than Khadijah, Muhammad later married her. About 610 CE, Muhammad heard what he believed were the words of God, whom he called Allah. He received many revelations from Allah and gradually gathered numerous followers who believed that Muhammad was a great prophet. These revelations were written down in a holy book called the Koran. The Koran served as a guide to a new religion called Islam, founded by Muhammad.

After Muhammad's death in 632 CE, his followers believed that he rose to heaven from the Temple Mount in Jerusalem, near the location of the Jewish Temple. Soon after Muhammad died, his followers, known as Muslims, joined together to form powerful armies. They conquered the entire Middle East, northern Africa, and even Spain, during the seventh and eighth centuries. After conquering Jerusalem, they built a great shrine called the Dome of the Rock at the Temple Mount, as well as a magnificent Muslim mosque—a house of worship. Nearby was all that remained of the Jewish Temple—a single wall, known as the Western Wall.

Jerusalem, which had been the center of the ancient Jewish homeland, had also become sacred to Muslims. Both sides—Jews and Muslims—believed that they were entitled to claim Jerusalem and the surrounding lands as their own.

## Jews and Muslims

During the Middle Ages, many Jews lived in Europe. They found themselves persecuted by Christians who held them responsible for the death of Jesus Christ. Jews were often prevented from owning land, and forced to live only in specific sections of European towns, which would be known as the Jewish Quarter. Some Jews, however, remained in Palestine, where they were respected by Muslims because of their ancient religion.

In Palestine, Jews formed a small community known as the Old Yishuv. The word *yishuv* means community. According to historian Arnold Blumberg, small communities of Jews existed not only in Jerusalem but in towns such as Tiberias, Hebron, and Safed. Some Jews rose to prominent positions under the Muslim leaders, or sultans, who ruled Palestine from Istanbul in present-day Turkey. During the sixteenth century, Joseph Nasi, a Jewish financier, became an important advisor to sultans Suleiman II and Selim, rulers of the large Ottoman Turkish Empire. By this time, the Muslims had been driven out of Spain by the Christians. Most Jews were also forced to leave the country because they would not convert to Christianity, and Nasi succeeded in resettling some of them in Palestine. In addition to these Jews, others came from Poland and Lithuania during the eighteenth and early nineteenth centuries.

## Life in the Turkish Empire

Most of the people in Palestine during the nineteenth century made their living from the land. Some of them were well-to-do families who owned large estates of more than one hundred acres. A few of them served as village chiefs, known as mukhtars, who were chosen from leading families. The Ottoman Turks relied on the mukhtars to collect taxes and appoint the watchmen who guarded each town and protected it from crime. While larger towns, such as Nablus, were walled, smaller ones had no walls for protection. Instead, villagers relied on thick stone houses with flat roofs, on which they stood and threw large stones down at would-be attackers.

Most of the farmers in the villages were poor peasants, known as fellaheen. They usually owned small plots of land that might produce just enough to support themselves. Many also had to work part-time on the estates of the well-to-do landowners to earn extra money. The farms in Palestine grew a variety of crops. These included wheat and corn, as well as olives that were turned into olive oil for cooking, and grapes that were used for wine making. The warm climate of Palestine was also excellent for growing oranges, which were shipped to Turkey, Egypt, and Western Europe.

Towns in Palestine were centers of manufacturing and exports. Many towns had a small olive press, where peasants brought their olives to be ground for oil or used in the manufacture of soap. Each town also had a flour mill where peasants brought their wheat to be ground into flour and made into bread.

Along the Mediterranean coast were larger cities, such as Haifa and Jaffa in southern Palestine. The small city of Jaffa was known as an export center. Merchants in Jaffa exported oranges grown in Palestine, as well as soap and wheat. Many shops opened in Jaffa between 1880 and 1910, and Muslims built beautiful mosques for prayer. As prices for food products rose during the nineteenth century, well-to-do landowners bought up more and more property. They turned this property into wheat fields and orange groves.

## Jews in Palestine

Well-to-do Muslims were not the only ones buying up land in Palestine. Wealthy European Jews also purchased land, hoping to help poor Jewish settlers escape the discrimination of Europe. In 1860, Sir Moses Montefiore set up a new settlement for Jews outside of Jerusalem. Born in Italy in 1784, Montefiore had moved to London where he became a very successful financier. He also married a member of the Rothschilds, another wealthy Jewish banking family. With some of his money, Montefiore sent financial aid to Jews in Russia.

During the 1880s, Russian Jews were victimized by pogroms—violence at the hands of Russian Christians who murdered Jews and destroyed their homes. These pogroms erupted after the assassination of Tsar Alexander II in 1881. The tsar had befriended the Jews and even permitted them to attend Russian universities, which had barred

Jewish students in the past. His successor, Alexander III, believed that somehow the Jews were involved in the murder of his father. The new tsar restricted the number of Jews allowed to enter universities. He helped create an atmosphere of renewed anti-Semitism across Russia. In this atmosphere, the pogroms broke out, and the Russian government did nothing to stop the violence.

Some Jews began to believe that the only way to deal with anti-Semitism was to find a place to settle outside of Europe. In 1882, a Russian Jew named Leo Pinsker published a pamphlet titled *Auto-Emancipation: A Warning of a Russian Jew to His Brethren*. He urged Jews to leave Russia for an area such as Palestine where they could live without anti-Semitism.

Palestine was the ancient Jewish homeland. Jews began leaving Russia to settle in Palestine—an emigration that would bring 25,000 settlers there over the next two decades. This became known as the First Aliya, a word that refers to the waves of migration.

In part, the First Aliya was inspired by the work of a Hungarian Jew named Theodor Herzl. In 1896, Herzl published a book titled *The Jewish State*, in which he wrote that the Jews would establish their own country within the next fifty years. In 1897, Herzl helped organize the First World Zionist Congress, bringing Jewish leaders together in Basel, Switzerland. Zion is another name for the Jewish homeland. Zionism refers to the effort aimed at establishing a Jewish homeland in Israel. The First Congress also discussed establishing a Jewish National Fund to provide financial support for bringing immigrants to Israel. This fund was finally set up in 1901, two years before a brutal pogrom broke out in Russia that killed forty-five Jews and injured hundreds of others. In 1904, a massive migration of Russian Jews, called the Second Aliya, swelled the Jewish population of Palestine. By 1914, the end of the Second Aliya, Jews comprised 10 percent, or 70,000, of the Palestinian inhabitants.

# Relations between Jews and Arabs in Palestine

Although Jews were only a small percentage of the Palestinian population, they were resented by some Arabs. The Arabs feared that Jews would try to reclaim their ancient homeland—an area that Muslims had developed over many centuries.

In 1891, Muslims in Jerusalem asked the Turkish ruler to limit the number of Jewish immigrants coming to Palestine. More than half of the new immigrants went to live in Jerusalem. Jews opened shops that competed with Arab merchants, causing them to fear that they might be forced out of business. Other Jewish immigrants bought up land, much of it from well-to-do Arab landowners. The Jews rapidly began tilling the soil with ploughs and fertilizing their crops with water pumps that were more efficient than Arab models.

According to Jewish historians Baruch Kimmerling and Joel Migdal, Jews claimed that their efficient methods improved farming for themselves as well as the Arabs. However, the Muslim farmers disagreed. They argued that Jews bought up property owned by Muslims and forced them off the land. Some Muslim farmers went to the cities looking for work. A few of them were employed by Jewish merchants, but, according to Kimmerling and Migdal, they were paid less than Jewish clerks. However, many Jewish businessmen refused to hire Arabs, preferring instead to provide jobs only for other Jews. Nevertheless, by 1914 the number of Jews in Palestine was still so small that many Arabs did not feel threatened by their presence. Indeed, many Jews and Muslims believed that all of them could live together in harmony.

## World War I

In August 1914, Jewish immigration to Palestine was cut short by the outbreak of World War I in Europe. The

Ottoman Turks were the allies of Germany and Austria-Hungary. They were involved in a brutal conflict against Great Britain, France, and Russia. Since the Russians were now their enemies, the Turks did not support any further immigration by Russian Jews to Palestine.

During the war, Great Britain tried to undermine the Turkish Empire in the Middle East. Many Arabs wanted to assert their independence from Turkey and establish their own nation, which might include Palestine as well as other areas. Among them was Emir Hussein, an Arab leader from Mecca, the birthplace of Muhammad in the present-day country of Saudi Arabia. The British encouraged Hussein to lead a revolt of the Arabs in the Middle East against the Turkish government. Hussein hoped to establish a new Arab nation, including Palestine. Meanwhile, Britain and France had negotiated a secret agreement planning to split up the Middle East between themselves after World War I had ended.

In the midst of these negotiations, the British had also been speaking to the Jews about a homeland in Palestine. As early as 1906, a Zionist leader, Dr. Chaim Weizmann, had met with one of England's leading politicians, Arthur James Balfour. Weizmann explained to Balfour that the Jews wanted Palestine as their homeland. Balfour wanted to know why the Jews wanted Palestine. "Mr. Balfour, supposing I were to offer you Paris instead of London, would you take it?" Dr. Weizmann asked. "But Dr. Weizmann," Balfour retorted, "we have London," to which Weizmann answered, "That is true, but we had Jerusalem when London was a marsh [long before it was established]." Jews regarded Jerusalem and Palestine as their homeland—the same area that Muslims believed belonged to them.

During World War I, Weizmann—a noted chemist—helped the British develop weapons to fight Germany. By

1917, the struggle against Germany and its allies had become more desperate. The Russian tsar had been over-thrown, taking an important British ally almost completely out of the war. Meanwhile, the United States had just recently entered the war against Germany. The English wanted to win over Jewish support in the new Russian government and keep it fighting for the Allies. They also wanted to thank Dr. Weizmann for his war efforts. Therefore, Balfour, who served as England's foreign minister, wrote a letter to Lord Walter Rothschild, an important Jewish leader in England. The letter contained the Balfour Declaration, issued November 2, 1917. It stated that the British government looked favorably on "the establishment in Palestine of a national home for the Jewish people, and will use their best endeavors to facilitate the achievement of this object."

When Arab leaders heard about the Balfour Declaration, they were stunned. However, the British assured them that the declaration also stated that "nothing shall be done which may prejudice the civil and religious rights of the non-Jewish communities in Palestine." In the meantime, British armies—with the help of the Arabs—overran the Turkish Empire in the Middle East. By 1918, Britain, France, and the United States had achieved victory, destroying the empires of Germany, Austria-Hungary, and the Ottoman Turks. According to treaties signed after the war, the Middle East was carved up into various territories. There was no large Arab empire. However, two of Hussein's sons were given control of present-day Jordan and Iraq. The British remained in charge of Palestine.

## British Palestine

In 1920, Great Britain appointed Herbert Samuel as the first high commissioner, in charge of the government in

Palestine. Born in 1870, Samuel had attended Oxford University. He entered politics during the 1890s, eventually winning election to the British Parliament and later serving in the British cabinet. Samuel was a Jew who had supported the Balfour Declaration. His appointment was welcomed by many Jewish settlers in Palestine who believed that the British promise for a Jewish national home in Palestine would be honored.

But Samuel also recognized that the British could only rule successfully if they provided equal treatment for both Arabs and Jews. Arabs believed that they had been promised Palestine by the British during World War I. Violence had already broken out early in 1920, when Arabs killed Jews at two settlements in northern Palestine. Bloodshed occurred again in April, when Arabs and Jews battled each other in Jerusalem.

This incident was created by one of the leading Palestinian Muslims, Muhammed Amin al-Husseini. He spoke to a large crowd of Arabs, urging them to take control of Palestine. As a result, Arabs attacked Jews who were praying at the Western Wall. Following the outbreak of violence, al-Husseini was arrested by the British. Nevertheless, he was freed by Commissioner Samuel early in 1922 and appointed Grand Mufti of Jerusalem—the religious leader of the Muslims in Palestine. In addition, al-Husseini was appointed head of the Supreme Muslim Council. This was an organization created by the British to govern the Palestinian Arabs and give them some local control over their own affairs.

Nevertheless, conflict between Arabs and Jews continued. The Grand Mufti began raising money to improve the Muslim shrines on the Temple Mount. However, Jews complained that they were being prevented from praying at the Western Wall. The Grand Mufti gave a speech to Arabs claiming that Jews had taken over the Muslim shrines. Although no takeover had occurred, violence started by the Arabs broke out in 1929 across Palestine, resulting in the deaths of 250 Arabs and Jews and more than 500 injuries.

Nevertheless, Jewish immigration into Palestine continued. Thousands of Jews came from Europe during the Third and Fourth Aliyas. Jews continued buying up farmland and opening new businesses. In the cities, young Muslim workers led strikes aimed at the British, who seemed to favor the Jews over the Arabs by permitting Jewish immigration. In 1933, a large demonstration of young Muslim Palestinians broke out in Jaffa against British rule. The government tried to stop the demonstrators, resulting in more than a dozen deaths.

By this time, many Jews realized that the conflict with the Muslims would continue and the British government could not stop it. In 1920, Jews had already formed a secret defense group known as the Haganah. Units of the Haganah were set up to defend Jewish towns and settlements. After the Arab demonstrations of 1929, however, the Haganah stepped up its operations. More and more young people and adults were trained to become members of the Haganah. The leaders of the Haganah purchased military supplies in Europe and began manufacturing their own weapons in Palestine. Many Jews who had hoped to create a new homeland that might include both Muslim and Jewish residents had gradually become convinced that peace was impossible. Meanwhile, Muslims were arming themselves with weapons obtained from neighboring Arab states.

The same realization had also come to the British government. In 1936, Great Britain issued the Peel Commission report. Led by William Robert Wellesley, Lord Peel, the commissioners called for a partition of Palestine into an Arab and a Jewish state. The new Arab state would include areas in the center of Palestine and in the north. The Jews would control a coastal area, roughly from Haifa to Jaffa, land around the Sea of Galilee, and the Negev

Desert. Jews were ready to accept the partition, but Arabs were not prepared to accept a Jewish state in Palestine.

The Peel report came amid violent demonstrations that had broken out among Arabs in the cities and across the countryside. The violence continued for two years. In 1937, the British drove out the Grand Mufti, one of the leaders of the Arab revolt. They also called on the assistance of the Haganah to help put down the violent demonstrations. In addition, British troops rounded up some Arab leaders, killed others, and destroyed Muslim homes. By 1939, the revolt had finally ended, but the Palestinian Arabs found themselves without any leadership.

## World War II

During the 1930s, Jews had also been dealing with another threat. In Germany, Nazi leader Adolf Hitler had begun a campaign of persecution against the Jews. They were prevented from voting, holding public office, or marrying non-Jews. On November 9, 1938, Nazi thugs attacked Jewish homes, shops, and synagogues in Germany and Austria, murdering innocent Jews who stood in their way. This pogrom was known as Kristallnacht—the night of broken glass.

As a result, Jewish immigration to Palestine from Germany grew during the Fifth Aliya in the 1930s. By 1939, 400,000 Jews lived in Palestine. Meanwhile, war was approaching between Germany and Great Britain. In the Middle East, the British wanted Arab support to help protect rich oil resources that might be essential to the war effort. In May 1939, the British government issued a new report, called the White Paper. It called for a reduction in Jewish immigration to Palestine, with an end to it in 1944, unless the Arabs agreed to admit more Jews. In addition, Great Britain backed the creation of an Arab state throughout Palestine.

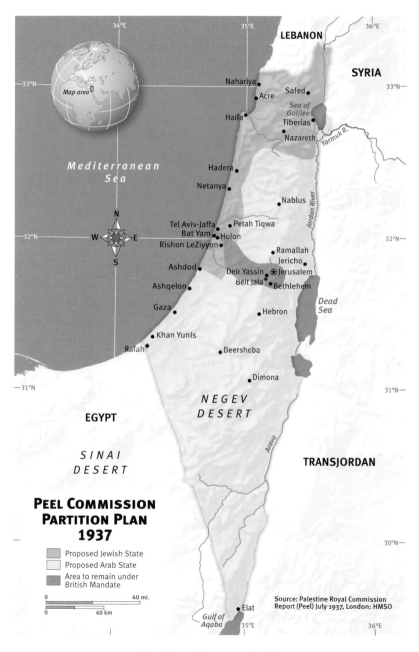

**PEEL COMMISSION PARTITION PLAN 1937**

- Proposed Jewish State
- Proposed Arab State
- Area to remain under British Mandate

Source: Palestine Royal Commission Report (Peel) July 1937, London: HMSO

**THE PEEL COMMISSION PLAN**

# Jewish Leaders in Palestine

Several Jewish leaders played key roles in the battle against Great Britain to establish a Jewish state. Among them was Menachem Begin. Born in Russia in 1913, Begin became a Zionist leader in Czechoslovakia and later Poland, helping Jews immigrate to Palestine. In 1943, Begin went to Palestine himself and joined the Irgun. He helped plan the attack on the King David Hotel in 1946.

Another radical leader was Avraham Stern. Born in Poland in 1907, Stern immigrated to Palestine in 1925 and became a member of the Haganah. After the riots in the late 1920s, Stern left the Haganah and helped create the more radical Irgun. Stern also wrote poetry, which inspired Jewish radicals in their fight against the British government in Palestine. During the late 1930s, Stern trained Irgun members to fight. However, he left the organization during World War II because most of the Irgun supported the British war effort to defeat the Nazis. Stern formed another group called the Fighters for the Freedom of Israel, also known as the Stern Gang. The Gang resorted to bank robbery as a way of supporting their efforts to undermine the British government. On February 12, 1942, British troops assaulted the house where Stern was hiding and killed him.

The best known Jewish leader during the fight for independence was David Ben-Gurion. Born in Poland in 1886, Ben-Gurion immigrated to Palestine in 1906. He helped establish the first Jewish kibbutz. This was a commune, where Jewish farmers worked together, shared equally in the crops they produced, and even shared ownership of their homes and furniture. During World War I, Ben-Gurion went to New York City, hoping to raise money for the Zionist efforts to establish a homeland. Later, he joined the Jewish Legion—an army unit that fought alongside the British during the war.

He also helped create the Histadrut, the Jewish national trade union in Palestine. This powerful union helped finance the Haganah. As head of the Jewish Agency from 1935, Ben-Gurion was recognized as the principal leader of the Zionist movement. He became the first prime minister of the new state of Israel in 1948.

War broke out in 1939, and German armies rapidly overran most of eastern and western Europe. Nazi leaders then began rounding up Jews and transporting them to concentration camps where they were killed. Very few were successful in escaping to Palestine, where British and Arab ships prevented Jews from landing. Nevertheless, Jews already living in Palestine fought side by side with the British, as Nazi forces tried to take control of the Middle East. Although Jews supported the British war effort against Nazi Germany, they did not give up their efforts to create a Jewish homeland. In May 1942, Jewish leaders met at the Biltmore Hotel in New York City, where they called for the establishment of a Jewish state after the war.

The defeat of the Nazis in 1945 revealed the full extent of the horrors endured by the Jews across Europe. More than six million had been killed by Nazis during the genocide—racial war—known as the Holocaust. The Jewish Agency, which had been established by the World Zionist Congress, called on the British to permit an additional 100,000 Jews into Palestine. This demand also received the support of U.S. President Harry Truman. However, the British were not prepared to allow a large new Jewish immigration that might threaten the position of the Palestinian Arabs.

On July 22, 1946, Jews struck back. The Haganah and a small radical group called the Irgun led a terrorist raid that struck the headquarters of the British government at the King David Hotel in Jerusalem. At 12:37 PM, a bomb exploded and reduced part of the hotel to rubble, killing almost one hundred people who worked for the government. Attacks by Jewish groups continued, and pressure mounted on the British to permit the creation of a Jewish state in Palestine. But the British were not prepared to back away from the White Paper issued in 1939.

Realizing that they could not bring peace to Palestine,

IN 1946, THE ZIONIST TERRORIST GROUP, THE IRGUN, BLEW UP THE KING DAVID HOTEL, WHERE THE BRITISH ARMY WAS HEADQUARTERED. NINETY-TWO PEOPLE DIED IN THE BLAST.

the British government finally announced in 1947 that it was prepared to give up control of the area. The British turned the problem over to the United Nations, the international organization that had been created at the end of World War II. A majority of the United Nations, including the United States, supported the partition of Palestine into two states—Arab and Jewish—according to U.N. Resolution 181. This decision led to increased conflict in Palestine. According to the plan, Jews received 55 percent of Palestine although they made up only 33 percent of the population.

# Israel and the Palestinians' Right of Return

Warfare has continued between Arabs and Jews for more than six decades. In 1948, the Jews acquired a nation that they named Israel. The United Nations also provided a homeland for Palestinians. But the Palestinians were forced to leave their homeland. For Palestinians, the right to return home has been at the center of their conflict with Israel ever since.

## Conflict over Partition

Muslims in Palestine were not prepared to accept the U.N. partition plan of 1947 set forth in Resolution 181. Strikes broke out among Muslim workers, followed by violence against Jewish shop owners. Muslims attacked Jewish neighborhoods in Jerusalem, where 100,000 Jews lived, as well as parts of Tel Aviv—a city founded by the Jews in 1909. About 325,000 Muslims lived in the areas the U.N. proposed to make into Israel.

Inside Palestine, however, there was little Arab leadership to coordinate attacks against the Jews. Although Palestinians numbered 1.3 million—more than twice the Jewish population—they had only tiny military units to

UNWILLING TO ACCEPT THE BRITISH PLAN FOR PARTITION OF PALESTINE, ARABS ATTACKED THE JEWS. HERE, AN ARAB SNIPING POST ON THE OLD CITY WALL IN JERUSALEM IS PICTURED. THE ARABS ARE SHOOTING TOWARD THE JEMIN MOSHE QUARTER, WHICH WAS INHABITED ALMOST EXCLUSIVELY BY JEWS IN 1948.

fight for an Arab state. Nevertheless, the Palestinians received assistance from the Arab League. Established in 1945, it included Egypt, Syria, Iraq, Transjordan [the present-day state of Jordan], Saudi Arabia, and Yemen. However, King Abdullah of Transjordan, the son of Sherif Hussein, was probably far more interested in acquiring the Arab sections of Palestine for his own nation rather than setting up an independent state. Nevertheless, in 1948, the league sent in the Arab Legion, consisting of about 8,000 troops, to fight against the Jews.

## Controversy over Deir Yassin

By March 1948, Jews and Muslims were fighting for control of the roads in Palestine. This conflict, known as the battle of roads, centered around the links between Tel Aviv on the

Mediterranean coast and Jerusalem. For a while, Jewish settlements in each city were almost cut off from each other by Arab military units. These units prevented food and water from reaching the Jews in Jerusalem. One of the strategic points along the road was the Arab village of Deir Yassin. In April an incident occurred at Deir Yassin, which, like many other elements of the long conflict between Muslims and Jews, is surrounded by controversy.

Approximately six hundred to seven hundred Muslims lived in the small village of Deir Yassin. According to some observers, Arab fighters wanted to establish a base of operations at Deir Yassin, which was just outside Jerusalem and south of the road connecting the city with Tel Aviv. However, the residents of Deir Yassin refused time after time to be involved in the warfare.

Some Jewish leaders, nevertheless, believed that Deir Yassin had become an important outpost in the battle for Jerusalem. Among them was Abba Eban, Israel's representative to the United Nations. Eban believed that Arab soldiers had taken control of Deir Yassin. Other Jewish leaders thought that in Deir Yassin, the soldiers of the Arab League were working together with local residents to cut the links between Tel Aviv and Jerusalem.

The attack on Deir Yassin by Jewish forces was spearheaded by members of the Irgun and the Stern Gang. Nevertheless, the operation had the approval of the leaders of the Haganah. Haganah intelligence officers had reported that Arab fighters were attacking vehicles along the roadway to Jerusalem and intercepting units of the Stern Gang.

Leading the operation was Menachem Begin, commander of the Irgun. His attack force included 132 soldiers. They assaulted Deir Yassin from two directions early in the morning of April 9, 1948. Jewish troops met fierce resistance from the Arabs in the villages, who included local residents as well as some members of the Arab League.

Jewish soldiers blew open the doors of houses with hand grenades and entered them, looking for the enemy. The Irgun had planned to bring a truck to the battle site with loudspeakers to broadcast a message to the villagers urging them to leave the town before the battle had begun.

Many villagers, however, did not leave Deir Yassin in time. By the end of the battle, about 120 residents—many of them innocent women and children—were dead. Historian Illan Pappe has called the incident at Deir Yassin a "massacre." He wrote that it was part of a master plan called Plan Dalet [D] designed to drive the Muslims out of Palestine. "The massacre in Deir Yassin played an important role in driving these groups out of Palestine in April and May 1948," he added, having "a psychological effect on the Arab community and acting as a catalyst to the exodus."

Menachem Begin told the story of Deir Yassin differently. He said that a vehicle with a loudspeaker had urged residents to leave the village but that they had not listened to the message. Historian Eric Silver wrote that while Begin may have wanted the message delivered, the truck with the loudspeaker was overturned in a ditch before ever transmitting the message.

## A New State Is Born

Meanwhile British troops were preparing to leave Palestine according to the terms of the U.N. partition plan of 1947. As the British withdrew, the Haganah battled Palestinian fighters for control of Palestinian towns and cities. The Haganah, which was far better organized than the Palestinians, gradually took control of Haifa and Jaffa. On May 14, 1948, Jewish leader David Ben-Gurion made an announcement to the world: "The Land of Israel was the birthplace of the Jewish people. Here, their spiritual, religious, and national identity was formed. Here they achieved independence and created a culture of national and universal significance. . . . We do hereby proclaim the establishment of the Jewish State in Palestine to be called the State of Israel."

The new state of Israel was immediately recognized by the United States as well as the Soviet Union (present-day Russia). However, it was still far from certain that Israel would survive. On May 15, Israel was invaded by Egypt, Syria, Lebanon, Iraq, and Transjordan. Although these troops totaled about 30,000, there was not much coordination between the various Arab nations. The main Israeli army, called the Israel Defense Force (IDF), also began receiving weapons from nations in Eastern Europe.

In May, Syrian forces advanced around the Sea of Galilee, but by fall 1948, they had been beaten back by the Israeli army. Egyptian armies advanced from the south through the Negev Desert, with infantry, artillery, and fighter planes. Uncoordinated attacks, combined with stout defense by Israeli settlers and IDF units, led to Egyptian defeats. The Egyptians were gradually pushed back and only succeeded in capturing a small area of the Negev known as the Gaza Strip. During fall 1948 and early 1949, Israeli forces occupied the rest of the desert area, including Eilat, at the southern end of the Negev. Eilat gave Israel a port on the Red Sea.

From the east, the armies of Transjordan and the Arab Legion occupied part of Jerusalem, known as the Old City. There was fierce house-to-house fighting, as the outnumbered Israelis gradually retreated. But a stiff Israeli defense prevented the Jordanians from capturing west Jerusalem, known as the New City.

In 1949, the United Nations intervened to bring peace to the region. Both sides were exhausted by the war. U.N. diplomats met with Israel and the Arab states on the Isle of Rhodes in the Mediterranean. According to agreements reached at Rhodes, the new state of Israel included a somewhat larger territory than the land included in the original partition agreement of 1947. However, no territory was given to the Palestinians for a new state. Nor did the Arab nations negotiate to give them a homeland. Instead, the rest of Palestine—the area along the West Bank of the Jordan River—went to Transjordan, which became known as the nation of Jordan. Jerusalem was split in half between Israel and Jordan.

## The Palestinian Right of Return

Since the 1948 war, Palestinians have believed that they were forced to leave their rightful homeland by the Jews. They also believe that they should be given the right to return home to Palestine. The departure of the Palestinians is an important issue that divides Arabs and Israelis.

Israelis believe that Palestinians were not forced to leave their homeland, but, frightened by war, left voluntarily. Many were scared away by the incident at Deir Yassin. As Begin himself put it, "Arabs throughout the country, induced to believe wild tales of 'Irgun butchery,' were seized with limitless panic and started to flee for their lives."

In the United States, many observers believed that the invasion by the Arab states led to the flight of the Palestinians and the end to their dream of an independent state. However, David Ben-Gurion has been quoted as supporting an effort to drive out the Palestinians. "The compulsory transfer of the Arabs from the valleys of the proposed Jewish state . . . could give us something which we never had . . . a real Jewish state—a contiguous, thickly populated agricultural bloc . . ." According to historian Cheryl Rubenberg, the purpose of Plan D was to give Israel all the territory allotted under the UN plan and even more. Plan D involved taking over Palestinian villages and cities and forcing out hundreds of thousands of Muslims.

By the time of the 1949 truce, most Palestinians had fled from the new state of Israel. A majority—approximately 600,000—went to the West Bank, Jordan, and Gaza, while others fled to Syria, Iraq, Lebanon, and Egypt. Palestinians called the 1948 war and their departure from Israel the Nakba, or the disaster.

Only about 150,000 Palestinians remained in Israel. Many were driven off their farms and forced to live in towns around the Sea of Galilee. Here the Israeli government could keep an eye on them to prevent a rebellion against the new nation. Not only were the Palestinians driven from their homes, they were prevented from moving out of their new locations to any other areas of Israel. Arabs were now a small, weakened minority in a nation controlled by Jews. They were kept under military rule until 1966.

The vast majority of Palestinians lived in makeshift refugee camps established in Gaza and the West Bank. At first, the Arabs lived only in tents, but gradually these were replaced by permanent stone houses. Many of the fellaheen were maintained by the relief efforts of the United Nations Relief and Works Agency (UNRWA). In Gaza, they received food supplies from UNRWA and some assistance from the Egyptian government that controlled the area. While many Arabs remained in the camps, where they became dependent on aid, the more educated Palestinians went to live in Gaza City where they found jobs in business. Palestinians dreamed of the day when they might avenge the loss of their homeland and take back control of Israel.

The majority of Palestinian refugees fled to the West Bank, where they became part of Jordan. Here conditions were similar to those in Gaza, but there were more towns and cities where educated Palestinians could find jobs. They went to east Jerusalem, for example, or Nablus, which became the center of Palestinian life on the West

# Death in Jerusalem

King Abdullah ibn Hussein of Jordan decided after 1948 to try to deal with the new Jewish state along his western border. When asked why he wanted peace with Israel, Abdullah explained: "I want peace not because I have become a Zionist or care for Israel's welfare, but because it is in the interest of my people. I am convinced that if we don't make peace . . . there will be another war, and another war, and another war, and we would lose." By 1951, there were twice as many Palestinians living in Jordan as native Jordanians. In July, King Abdullah traveled to Jerusalem to pray at the al-Aqsa mosque at the Temple Mount. Unknown to most people, the sixty-nine-year-old Abdullah also planned a secret meeting with members of the Israeli government. Abdullah was joined by his grandson, sixteen-year-old Hussein.

Before leaving for Jerusalem, Abdullah had told an aide, "When I have to die, I would like to be shot in the head by a nobody. That's the simplest way of dying." On July 20, 1951, Abdullah and his grandson arrived in Jerusalem and entered the al-Aqsa mosque at the Temple Mount. Moments later, the king was approached by a lone gunman who fired a shot and killed him. Hussein himself was spared because a bullet from the assassin's gun hit a medal on his uniform.

The assassin had been hired by Haj Amin al-Husseini, the Grand Mufti. Many Palestinians, like the Mufti, were opposed to any kind of agreement with Israel and hated King Abdullah for even suggesting peace. King Abdullah was briefly succeeded by his son, who was mentally unstable. But in 1952, Hussein became king of Jordan—a position he held until his death in 1999.

Bank. Some Palestinians also became involved in guerrilla activities, which were being launched against the state of Israel from inside Jordan.

## The Approach of War at Suez

Raids were not only occurring along the West Bank but also along the Israeli border with Egypt. In 1952, Egyptian military leaders, calling themselves the Free Officers, had overthrown the corrupt government of King Farouk, which had been too weak to defeat the Jews in the war of independence. The Free Officers reorganized the government, and by 1956 one of the officers, Gamal Abdul-Nasser, had become president of Egypt.

Born in 1918 in a suburb of Alexandria, Egypt, Nasser later said that he was "proud to be a member of a poor family." Nasser attended high school and was admitted to the Egyptian military college, which had begun accepting students from poor families during the 1930s. After graduation, Nasser joined a military unit where he met Anwar El Sadat (the future Egyptian president who succeeded Nasser). Nasser served in Egyptian forces during the 1948 war. As he put it: "We were fighting in Palestine, and our dreams were in Egypt. Our bullets were targeting the enemy but our hearts were with our nation who was left for the wolves." After the war, Nasser and Sadat helped ignite the revolution that overthrew King Farouk. Indeed, Sadat announced the victory over Egyptian radio.

Nasser dreamed of reasserting Arab power in the Middle East, which involved restoring the Palestinians to their homelands and defeating the Israelis. In 1955, Nasser made a deal with the Soviet Union to receive planes and tanks in return for Egyptian cotton. At the same time, he was trying to persuade the United States to finance a huge dam that would improve irrigation for Egyptian farmers and provide hydroelectric power. When the United States

**EGYPTIAN PRESIDENT GAMAL ABDUL NASSER IS CHEERED BY A HUGE CROWD ON HIS ARRIVAL BACK IN CAIRO FROM ALEXANDRIA, WHERE HE ANNOUNCED THAT HE HAD TAKEN OVER THE MANAGEMENT OF THE SUEZ CANAL.**

pulled out of the deal, Nasser retaliated by taking over the Suez Canal. This waterway was designed by French engineers and built by Egyptians from 1859 to 1869 to connect the Mediterranean with the Red Sea. It was a critical link between the Middle East and India—a colony of Great Britain. Indeed, the British purchased a major interest in the canal during the latter part of the nineteenth century. Both France and Great Britain had run the canal until 1956, when it was taken over by Nasser, who regarded a European presence in Egypt as an insult to Arab nationalism.

While Nasser's action was widely supported in Egypt and throughout the Arab world, the French and British were not willing to lose control of the Suez Canal. Meanwhile, the Israeli government regarded Egypt's new weapons as a direct threat to the Jewish nation. Nasser had also decided to close the Straits of Tiran, stopping

Israeli ships from entering the Red Sea from the Jewish port of Eilat on the Gulf of Aqaba. Nasser's action violated the agreements signed by Israel and the Arab nations following the War of Independence. In 1955, Nasser had also signed a joint military agreement with Syria that seemed aimed at surrounding and destroying Israel.

High Israeli government officials, including Foreign Minister Golda Meir and IDF chief of staff Moshe Dayan, were holding secret meetings with French and British officials in Paris. Together they developed a plan that called for a lightning strike by the Israeli army across the Sinai Desert toward the Suez Canal. As the IDF approached the canal, the French and British would intervene, supposedly to protect Suez from falling to Israel, but actually to take back control of the waterway.

Late in the afternoon of October 29, 1956, Israeli paratroopers took control of the Mitla Pass through the hills in the Sinai Desert. As a result, Egyptian forces in the desert were cut off from reinforcements in the area around Suez.

Meanwhile, Israeli tanks and soldiers defeated Egyptian forces holding Abu Ageila, Rafah, and Gaza City. Other units rapidly headed south and took Sharm El-Sheikh, the Egyptian city at the southern end of the Gulf of Aqaba—opening up access to the Red Sea. In early November, as the IDF approached the Suez Canal, France and Britain began their attacks.

But at this point the United States intervened, along with the Soviet Union, warning the French and British forces to stop their invasion. Israel was also forced to give up the territory it had won in the Sinai Desert. Nevertheless, the Israelis won a guarantee from the United Nations to take over control of Gaza as well as Sharm El-Sheikh. This would reduce guerrilla attacks from Gaza and enable Israel to retain access to the Red Sea.

# The Six Day War

Over the next decade, conditions between Israel and the surrounding Arab states did not improve. In 1958, Egypt and Syria established the United Arab Republic (UAR), with President Nasser in control of the new government. This not only increased Nasser's power in the Middle East, but also represented a unified threat to Israel along its southern and northern borders. However, the Syrians rapidly grew tired of taking orders from Nasser, and the UAR ended late in 1961.

However, Jordan continued its secret meetings with the Israelis, trying to improve relations along the West Bank. In September 1963, according to historian Roland Dallas, King Hussein held a meeting with a representative of Israeli Prime Minister Levi Eshkol. He also met with Foreign Minister Meir. However, Hussein had to move very carefully. Palestinians still dreamed of returning to Israel and viewed any effort by King Hussein to negotiate with the Jews as a betrayal. Hussein was also aware that his powerful neighbors, Syria and Egypt, were violently opposed to the existence of Israel and might even send agents into Jordan to undermine Hussein's government. Indeed, the king was the target of numerous assassination attempts throughout his long reign.

Meanwhile, President Nasser had rebuilt his army with numerous tanks and planes supplied by the Soviet Union. On May 8, 1967, the Soviets told Nasser and the Syrians that Israel was planning a surprise attack. Although there was no evidence to back up this claim, Nasser believed it and began to mobilize his soldiers in the Sinai Desert. At the same time he ordered the United Nations' small peacekeeping force to evacuate Gaza and Sharm el-Sheikh. Nasser also blocked the Gulf of Aqaba to Israeli ships. This was a violation of international law. All these acts sent a signal to Israel that seemed to suggest that war was coming.

Did Nasser actually intend a war? Certainly the Israeli government thought so. But historian Roland Dallas disagrees. On June 2, he quoted Nasser as saying, "We have no intention of attacking Israel." King Hussein agreed: "I don't think the Egyptian president wanted to come to actual war. I even suspect that he didn't really believe war would break out. In my view it was inescapable."

Hussein himself did not want war with Israel, but he felt trapped. He was afraid that if he didn't join the other Arab countries, Jordan would be "branded as a traitor to the Arab cause."

As Jewish leader Chaim Herzog wrote, "Israel was soon ringed by a [huge] Arab force. . . . The world looked on at what was believed by many to be the impending destruction of Israel." Herzog said that Prime Minister Ben-Gurion had decided to go to war in 1956 after an alliance was formed between Egypt and Syria. Now the Arabs had formed a similar alliance. "Furthermore," Herzog wrote, "the Government of Israel had frequently made it clear that the blocking of the Straits of Tiran would be interpreted by Israel as an active declaration of war by the Arab countries."

## War Begins

Under the direction of IDF Chief of Staff Yitzhak Rabin, Israel prepared to launch a pre-emptive strike—an attack designed to surprise the enemy before they could assault Israel. Early in the morning of June 5, 1967, Israeli planes took off, headed for Egypt. While Egyptian planes stood on the runways, Israeli jets attacked and bombed most of the Egyptian aircraft, destroying them. The Egyptian air force had been knocked out of the war before the conflict had really begun. Meanwhile, the IDF swept across the

Sinai Desert in a repeat of the 1956 war. Egyptian military units were rapidly driven backward, giving up Gaza City, Rafah, and Abu Ageila. Masses of Egyptian tanks tried to retreat through the Mitla Pass, where they were destroyed by the Israeli aircraft. Israeli forces drove through the pass and advanced along the Mediterranean coast, taking up a position just east of the Suez Canal. There was little the Egyptians could do to stop them.

In the north, King Hussein had been told by Nasser that the Egyptians were winning the war against Israel. Meanwhile, the Israeli government had sent a message to Hussein saying that the IDF would not attack his positions on the West Bank if he stayed out of the war. But Hussein felt that he was obligated to help his allies. So he began to prepare his attack against west Jerusalem. His planes made a small attack against Israeli airfields, doing little damage, and returned to Jordan. While they were sitting on the runways, they were destroyed by Israeli bombers, who had already finished off the Egyptian air force.

Nevertheless, fierce fighting broke out between the Jordanian Arab Legion and the IDF along the West Bank and around Jerusalem. The Jordanians were outnumbered and they could not receive any reinforcements from inside Jordan because the supply lines were being heavily bombed by the Israeli Air Force. By June 7, the IDF had taken control of the entire city of Jerusalem, and the West Bank had also fallen into Israeli hands.

Northward, fighting had also broken out along the Golan Heights on the border between Israel and Syria. For years, the Syrians had shelled Israeli settlements from artillery positions along the Golan Heights. At the beginning of the war, Syrian planes attacked oil refineries in the Israeli city of Haifa. The Israeli air force retaliated, knocking out almost all of the Syrian planes. On June 9, the IDF began an attack on the Syrian positions along the Golan. After a bloody battle that led to heavy casualties on both sides, the Syrians finally retreated, leaving the IDF in command of the Golan Heights.

## Six Day War: The Seeds of the Present Conflict

Israelis viewed the Six Day War as a tremendous military victory. The West Bank, which had pushed itself into the Israeli midsection, had been eliminated. Israel had gained a large piece of territory that prevented Jordanian guns on the West Bank from shelling Israeli positions in Tel Aviv along the coast. By taking the West Bank—which Jews called Judea and Samaria—Israel had also retaken what was considered part of the ancient Jewish homeland. In the north, the Syrian positions along the Golan Heights had been destroyed, creating a much safer position for Israeli settlements near the border with Syria. In the south, Israel had picked up the vast Sinai, which contained enormous oil resources. The Israeli government had also taken control of Sharm al-Sheikh and pushed back the Egyptian borders to the Suez Canal. These gains improved Israeli defenses.

For Palestinians, however, the Six Day War seemed to put an end to any immediate hopes that they could return to Palestine. Israel was stronger than ever. Jews had acquired land that included the homes of many Palestinians. Indeed, the Six Day War created a new Nakba for the Palestinians. Approximately 300,000 of them became refugees. They fled from the West Bank and Gaza to Jordan and Egypt. Some were forcibly removed by the Israelis from East Jerusalem and taken to Jordan.

The Israelis have remained in control of the West Bank until the present. This has sharpened the conflict between Palestinians and Israelis. It has increased demands by the Palestinians for the right to return to their former homelands—more of which were lost in the 1967 war. Soon after the end of the war, Israelis began to place new settlements on the West Bank. They intended, just as strongly as the Palestinians, to claim this land as their own and make it a permanent part of Israel.

## The Six Day War and the Arab States

Among the Arab nations, the Six Day War was considered a complete disaster. Three years after the war ended, President Nasser died of a heart attack and was succeeded by his vice president, Anwar Sadat. But Sadat later said that

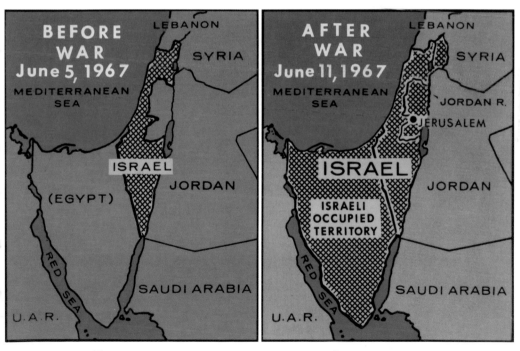

**THESE MAPS SHOW THE TERRITORIES HELD BY ISRAEL BEFORE AND AFTER THE SIX DAY WAR IN JUNE 1967.**

**PALESTINIANS FLED FROM ISRAEL TO JORDAN DURING THE SIX DAY WAR.**

"the events of 5 June dealt him a fatal blow. They finished him off. Those who know Nasser realized that he did not die on September 28, 1970, but on 5 June 1967, exactly one hour after the war broke out [when the Egyptian air force was destroyed]. That was how he looked at the time, and for a long time afterwards—a living corpse. The pallor of death was evident on his face and hands, although he still moved and walked, listened and talked."

After the Six Day War, the United Nations Security Council passed Resolution 242. It called for Israel to withdraw from "territories occupied in the recent conflict." In turn, every nation in the Middle East was called on to respect the "sovereignty, territorial integrity, and political independence of every State in the area." Unfortunately, Israel and the surrounding Arab states could not agree on what Resolution 242 meant. Arabs believed that Israel must return all the territory conquered in the war in return for having its sovereignty respected. Israel, however, interpreted Resolution 242 to mean that the Israelis would only be required to negotiate new national boundary lines with the Arab states once they agreed to peace with Israel.

Israel even offered to return the Sinai to Egypt and the Golan Heights to Syria in return for peace. But at a meeting in Khartoum, Sudan, on September 1, Arab leaders gave a blunt response. They answered with three "no's": no peace, no negotiation, no recognition of Israel. Israel's victory in the Six Day War had only worsened relations between Israel and the surrounding Arab states, just as it had between Israelis and Palestinians.

# Yasir Arafat
# Leads the PLO

The events of 1967 had been a complete disaster for many Arab leaders. But there was one exception. His name was Yasir Arafat.

Abd al-Rahman Abd al-Rauf Arafat al-Qudwa al Husseini was born in Cairo, Egypt, on August 24, 1929. One of seven children, he was nicknamed Yasir, which means "easygoing." When he was five, Arafat's mother died and for a short time he was sent to live with his uncle in Jerusalem. Although Arafat would later claim that he was born in Jerusalem—the center of the Palestinian struggle for a homeland—he was actually Egyptian. As Barry Rubin and Judith Colp Rubin have written, "Everything is controversial when it comes to Yasir Arafat, even the question of where his life began."

While Arafat lived in Jerusalem, he may have witnessed the bloody riots that were part of the Palestinian uprising of 1935–1936. By 1940, Arafat had returned to his father's home in Cairo. Then, according to Arafat's own account, he returned to Jerusalem and participated in the 1948 war that led to the establishment of Israel and the defeat of the Palestinians. Arafat may have worked for the

EVEN THE YOUNGEST PALESTINIANS ARE TRAINED IN THE FIGHT
AGAINST THE ISRAELI OCCUPIERS. HERE, A YOUNG GIRL IS SHOWN
HOLDING A MACHINE GUN. SHE AND THE OTHER CHILDREN ARE BEING
TRAINED AS COMMANDOS AT A PALESTINIAN REFUGEE CAMP.

Grand Mufti. "I was in Jerusalem when the Zionists tried
to take over the city and make it theirs," Arafat later said.
He also claimed to have escaped through the village of
Deir Yassin, the site where many Palestinian women and
children were killed. But according to historian Efraim
Karsh, Arafat was actually in Cairo attending high school.

In 1949, Arafat began attending King Faud University
in Cairo, where he studied engineering. Outside the university, Arafat received training by the Muslim Brotherhood, a
militant Egyptian group that wanted to drive the British
out of the Suez Canal. Whether or not Arafat actually participated in guerrilla activities carried on by the Brotherhood against the British is open to question. According to
King Faud University, he was in engineering class.

After graduating from Faud University, Arafat took a job as an engineer building roads in Kuwait—a small, oil-rich country in the Middle East. When he was not laying out roadways, Arafat spent his time with young men who had already committed themselves to driving the Jews out of Palestine. Among them was Khalil al-Wazir—who later called himself Abu Jihad. His family had left Palestine during the 1948 war. Arafat's other friends included Khalid al-Hasan and Faruq Qaddumi, who had also lost their homeland during the war. Together these men formed the Palestinian Liberation Movement on October 10, 1959. The Movement was nicknamed Fatah, an Arab acronym that stands for Palestine Liberation Movement.

According to Arafat, Fatah was dedicated to retaking Palestine. "We have only one motto: Victory or death," he said. Instead of political leaders, he added, "It is the commandos who will decide the future." Arafat himself had already begun looking the part of a commando. He had a stubbly beard and wore a holstered pistol, as well as a kaffiyeh, or head scarf. These became the hallmarks of his appearance until his death in 2004. As head of Fatah, Arafat began touring the countries of the Middle East looking for money to support guerrilla activities against Israel.

## The PLO

Meanwhile, Egyptian President Gamal Abdul Nasser had decided to put greater emphasis on the plight of the Palestinian refugees. In 1964, he supported the establishment of the Palestine Liberation Organization (PLO). The PLO was organized by a group of Palestinian leaders meeting in east Jerusalem, then part of Jordan. The PLO included a legislature, known as the Palestine National Council, an army, and a chairman named Ahmad Shuqeiri, a strong ally of Nasser. It was dedicated to establishing a government in Gaza and on the West Bank—and to destroying Israel.

# Yasir Arafat and Gamal Abdul Nasser

Yasir Arafat and Gamal Abdul Nasser conducted an historic meeting in Egypt in April 1968. Arafat arrived at the meeting wearing both his well-known kaffiyeh—a traditional checked, cloth headgear—as well as a pistol. At first, Nasser's security police were not going to permit Arafat to enter the meeting. They were afraid that he might be a threat to Nasser. However, Nasser decided that it was all right for Arafat to remain armed while they talked. "My intelligence people are telling me that you insist on bringing your gun because you intend to kill me," Nasser said. Arafat took off the gun and handed it to him.

"Mr. President, your intelligence people are wrong. I offer you my freedom fighter's gun as proof of that fact." Nasser had a ready answer for the guerrilla leader. "No. You keep it. You need it and more. I would be more than glad if you could represent the Palestinian people and the Palestinian will to resist, politically by your presence and militarily by your actions."

Nasser and Arafat became allies. Following the meeting between Arafat and Nasser, the Egyptian leader announced that he was ready to provide financial backing to Fatah. He also put Arafat in charge of the *Voice of Palestine* Radio in Cairo. Nasser also took Arafat on a trip to Moscow. There, Arafat was introduced to the Soviet leaders who were backing the Arabs in their struggle against Israel.

Arafat and Fatah did not join the PLO. Instead they decided to carry on guerrilla activities against Israel. From headquarters in Damascus, Syria, Fatah launched attacks on Israeli targets during 1965. Fatah tried to set up another base of operations in Gaza, but their members were arrested by the Egyptians. They regarded Fatah as a threat to the PLO. Nasser feared that guerrilla attacks against Israel might touch off another war with the Jewish state before the Arab states were ready to launch their own war.

When that war finally came in 1967, it ended in disaster. The PLO and Shuqueiri, as allies of Nasser, immediately lost credibility. As Barry Rubin and Judith Colp Rubin wrote, "While the war was a catastrophe for both the Arab regimes and the PLO, it provided Arafat's great opportunity. He had been advocating an alternative strategy of guerrilla war and questioning an exclusive reliance on the Arab states and conventional military forces to destroy Israel. Many now thought that events had proved Arafat to be correct."

After the 1967 war ended, Arafat went to Egypt for a meeting with Nasser. There the Egyptian president promised to support Arafat and ensure that he would become the next leader of the PLO. In February 1969, at a meeting of the Palestine National Council, Arafat was selected as the new chairman of the Palestine Liberation Organization.

## Guerrilla War against Israel

From bases on the West Bank, Arafat directed guerrilla activities against Israel, often killing innocent children. These attacks were met with counterattacks by the Israelis. Some of them were led by General Ariel Sharon—one of the Israeli leaders who had won the Six Day War. This was the beginning of the personal conflict between Sharon and Arafat.

Many Palestinians on the West Bank, however, seemed to have little interest in battling the Israelis.

Some had found work in Israel and had no interest in undermining the government. Others favored establishing a new Palestinian state on the West Bank and in Gaza. These areas were rapidly improving economically. However, Arafat was completely opposed to the idea. Instead, he wanted to drive out King Hussein and take over Jordan—at least this is what the king believed, according to Roland Dallas.

King Hussein feared that the stability of his own country might be jeopardized and tried to reach an agreement with Arafat. But Arafat continued to plot against the Jordanians. On September 6, the Popular Front for the Liberation of Palestine (PFLP)—a small faction of the PLO—hijacked two American airliners and one Swiss plane. Two of the planes were taken to Jordan, where the PFLP terrorists were surrounded by the Jordanian army. King Hussein then decided that he could no longer tolerate the PLO in Jordan because it represented a threat to the future of his government. On September 17, 1970, Jordanian troops marched on PLO positions in Amman, the capital of Jordan. Arafat and his associates called this attack Black September. By early 1971, the PLO and its leader had been driven out of Jordan. Fleeing to Lebanon, they established a new base of operations.

## The PLO in Lebanon

From Beirut, the capital of Lebanon, the PLO began to launch new attacks—not only at Israel but at others who opposed the Palestinian cause. In 1971, Arafat founded a new group called Black September, aimed at destabilizing the Jordanian government. On November 28, Wasfi al-Tal, Jordan's prime minister, was assassinated at the Sheraton Hotel in Cairo.

In 1972, Black September infiltrated the living quarters of Israeli athletes at the Olympic Games in Munich, Germany. The athletes were removed from their rooms at gunpoint, taken to a bus by Black September terrorists, and driven to a nearby airport. As police tried to stop the getaway, the terrorists set off a bomb, destroying the bus, killing themselves and many of the Israeli hostages. Early the following year, Black September struck again. This time, they attacked a diplomatic party in Khartoum, Sudan. Cleo Noel, the United States ambassador, as well as other officials, were kidnapped by the terrorists. Noel, her assistant, as well as other diplomats, were murdered by the Black September gunmen before the latter finally surrendered to authorities. "There was little doubt in anyone's mind that the decision [to kill the American diplomats] went right back to Arafat," said a high-ranking American intelligence official. "The U.S. government had evidence of his involvement in the go-ahead."

## The Coming Conflict

While Arafat was directing guerrilla activities, Israel and the surrounding Arab states were preparing for another war. After the close of the 1967 war, Israel had built a defense line along the Suez Canal. Called the Bar-Lev Line for IDF Chief of Staff Chaim Bar-Lev, it included massive, fortified posts. These were designed to protect Israeli troops against Egyptian artillery. Artillery duels frequently broke out around the Suez Canal, and Israeli and Egyptian jet fighter planes carried on dogfights thousands of feet in the air. This conflict, known as the War of Attrition, continued for three years, until Israel and Egypt finally agreed to a peace treaty. Shortly after the ceasefire in August 1970, President Sadat began rebuilding the military power of Egypt so he could launch a new strike against Israel.

Unlike the 1967 war, Sadat's plan included only limited objectives. He proposed that his armies should cross the Suez Canal, overrun the Bar-Lev Line, and push the Israelis back into the Sinai Desert. During the attacks,

Egyptian missiles would knock down Israeli aircraft. Meanwhile, the Syrians would attack Israel from the north, trying to regain control of the Golan Heights. As the IDF tried to dislodge the Egyptians and the Syrians, Sadat expected that the Soviets and the United States would stop the war. The Soviets backed the Arabs, while the United States was allied with Israel. Neither the Soviets nor the United States wanted to see their allies defeated. The Arab victory would increase their prestige and might prompt Israel to give back territory that had been taken during the Six Day War.

President Sadat was planning an actual attack for October 6, 1973. This was Yom Kippur, the most important holy day in the Jewish religion. Sadat hoped to take Israel completely by surprise while its citizens were absorbed with religious worship. Meanwhile, Israeli intelligence reported that the possibility of war was "the lowest of the low." Sadat's surprise had worked.

## Yom Kippur War

Egyptian forces launched a massive attack on October 6, overrunning the lightly defended Bar-Lev Line. While the initial assault caught the IDF unprepared, they quickly mobilized the reserve units and began sending reinforcements into the Sinai. By October 9, Israeli tank units had succeeded in stopping the Egyptian advance and a stalemate began along the battlefield.

Meanwhile in the north, Syrian troops attacked Israeli positions on the Golan Heights. At first, the Syrian tanks and infantry, like their Egyptian allies, were successful in driving back the Israelis. But the IDF units put up a fierce resistance. An Israeli tank commander of the 188 IDF Brigade, Zwicka Gringold, used his four tanks—known as Force Zwicka—to defend a road against a much larger force of Syrians. Three of his tanks were put out of action.

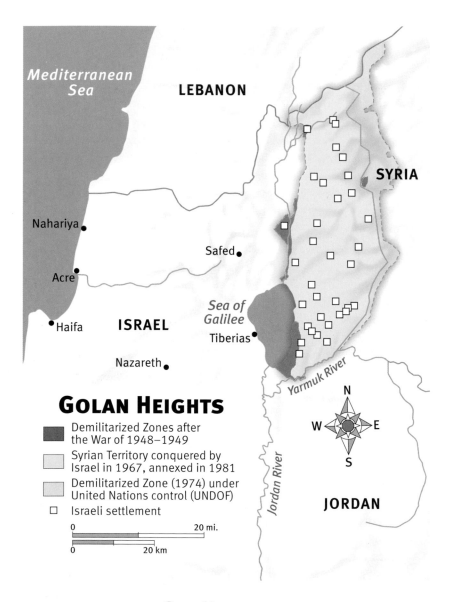

GOLAN HEIGHTS

- Demilitarized Zones after the War of 1948–1949
- Syrian Territory conquered by Israel in 1967, annexed in 1981
- Demilitarized Zone (1974) under United Nations control (UNDOF)
- □ Israeli settlement

0 ——————— 20 mi.
0 ——————— 20 km

**GOLAN HEIGHTS**

But Gringold, commanding the fourth tank, kept firing at the Syrian forces until he was finally forced to retreat. After the battle he received the Order of Courage, the highest award given by the Israeli government for courage under fire.

Israeli reserves were rushed into the Golan. By October 10, an Israeli counterattack was under way that gradually drove the Syrians back from their positions. The IDF then began to advance into Syria.

Meanwhile, in the south, a massive tank battle occurred east of the Suez Canal between Egyptian and Israeli forces. More than 2,000 tanks were engaged, but this time the Egyptians were driven back by superior Israeli power. As the Egyptians retreated, a large hole opened in their lines and the IDF decided to exploit it. Israeli tanks, led by General Ariel Sharon, pushed through the Egyptian line. On October 15, Sharon began crossing the Suez Canal into Egypt. So successful was the Israeli breakthrough that part of the Egyptian Third Army on the east side of the Suez Canal in the Sinai was cut off from its base in Egypt.

At this point, President Sadat begged the Soviet Union to step in and call for a meeting with the United States to bring about a ceasefire. On October 22, the United Nations Security Council, led by the United States and the Soviet Union, passed Resolution 338, bringing a ceasefire. The United Nations then sent a small force to the Middle East. Its job was to patrol the area between the two sides so the ceasefire would continue. In addition, the IDF permitted a U.N. food convoy to provide supplies to the soldiers of the trapped Third Army.

The Yom Kippur War had finally ended. Both sides claimed victory. Israel had pushed the Syrians back from the Golan Heights and invaded Syria. The IDF had also surrounded the Egyptian Third Army. Sadat, however, had surprised the Israelis with his attack across the canal. The

Egyptians had also succeeded in overrunning the Bar-Lev Line and regaining territory in the Sinai Desert lost during the Six Day War. The controversy over the results of the war—who won and who lost—became part of the larger conflict between Israel and the Arabs.

# The United States, Israel, and the Arabs

For many years, the United States and the Soviet Union were the world's two superpowers. Both nations had nuclear weapons capable of destroying the entire planet. Throughout the world, they maintained an uneasy balance of power. Each side had its own allies in various parts of the globe, including the Middle East. President Harry Truman supported the partition of Palestine and gave U.S. recognition to the new state of Israel in 1948. President Truman believed that Jews should have a homeland, especially after the horrors they had endured during the Holocaust in World War II. In the nineteenth and twentieth centuries, many Jews had immigrated to the United States from Europe. In the United States they formed an important voting group that lobbied very hard in favor of the new state of Israel.

While the United States backed Israel, the Soviet Union supported Egypt and other Arab states. The Soviets supplied Egypt and Syria with weapons during the 1960s. The United States, on the other hand, provided military supplies to Israel. After Nasser and the other Arab states were defeated in the 1967 war, the United States intervened. After

Richard M. Nixon was elected president in 1968, his secretary of state, William Rogers, introduced a plan that led to a ceasefire between Israel and Egypt in 1970. The United States and the Soviet Union worked together to bring about a ceasefire after the Yom Kippur War.

## The Results of the 1973 War

While Israel had been the clear victor in the 1967 war, the results of the 1973 conflict were different. Egypt had achieved at least a limited success. Meanwhile, Israelis realized that their nation was not unbeatable. Their armies had been pushed back and suffered serious losses. Indeed, the fact that Israel was surprised by the Egyptian attack led to the resignation of Israeli Prime Minister Golda Meir. She was replaced by Yitzhak Rabin. General Rabin had engineered the Israeli victory in 1967, and had been serving as ambassador to the United States in 1973. Therefore, he was not blamed for Israel's lack of preparedness in the Yom Kippur War.

Against this situation in Israel and Egypt, the United States intervened to broker a peace settlement. This time U.S. Secretary of State Henry Kissinger began a round of talks that eventually led to an agreement. Kissinger's mission was critical to the West. Arab states had unleashed a new weapon during the 1973 war. Led by oil-rich Saudi Arabia, Arab states had drastically reduced their supplies of oil to nations such as the United States. King Faisal of Saudi Arabia stated that the embargo would remain in effect unless the United States pressured the Israelis to leave their positions along the canal and give the Palestinians a homeland. As a result, the United States urgently needed to bring about a settlement that would rescue the Egyptian Third Army from the grasp of the IDF and move Israeli soldiers out of Egypt.

Talks had actually begun between Israeli and Egyptian

representatives late in October 1973. They took place in the Sinai Desert at Kilometer 101 and were called the KM 101 discussions. Meanwhile, Kissinger arrived in Cairo and began his meetings with President Sadat. The two men seemed to understand each other and cooperate from the beginning. "We began our meeting with caution in what we had to say," Sadat later explained, "but after an hour of discussion I was convinced that Kissinger was a man to be trusted; he spoke logically, his perspective was clear."

Diplomatic talks continued over the next several months. Kissinger shuttled back and forth between Israel and Egypt. This process, which became known as shuttle diplomacy, led to an agreement in January 1974. Israel agreed to withdraw 15 miles (9 km) from the Suez Canal. In return President Sadat promised to reduce Egyptian military forces on the east side of the canal. Sadat also worked to persuade the Saudis to resume shipping oil to the United States and its Western allies.

Meanwhile, Kissinger was also conducting shuttle diplomacy between Israel and Syria. This finally led to an agreement that kept Israel in control of most of the Golan Heights, except for a small area controlled by the Syrians. However, the Syrian and Egyptian agreements had no provisions for the Palestinians. This element, called "linkage," was supposed to link any deal with Israel to the Israelis' complete withdrawal from all territory occupied after the 1967 war. The Arab states had publicly announced their support for the return of all Palestinian refugees to their homeland in Israel.

## Yasir Arafat and the PLO

Nevertheless, the PLO had not been forgotten. According to historian Roland Dallas, Yasir Arafat had "traveled the world, Arab and non-Arab, seeking support for the Palestinians' cause. He was persuasive. . . . It was murmured in the [Middle East] that at times the PLO's requests for money were, if not threatening, heavy-handed."

In October 1974, Arafat was invited to speak before the United Nations in New York. There he said that he was "bearing an olive branch and a freedom fighter's gun. Do not let the olive branch fall from my hand," he warned the delegates at the United Nations General Assembly.

At a meeting of Arab states in October 1974, the PLO was recognized as "the sole legitimate representative of the Palestinian people" with authority over all Palestinian territory. Therefore, any land on the West Bank given up by Israel would not be controlled by Jordan but by the PLO. However, Israel had no intention of giving up any of this land. Many Israelis viewed it as part of their original, Biblical homeland. In fact, Israelis had already planted their own settlements on the West Bank.

In the Sinai, however, Kissinger had brokered a second agreement by 1975 (Sinai II). He persuaded the Israelis to withdraw even farther eastward. United Nations peacekeepers were placed in between the Egyptian and Israeli forces. The United States established electronic monitoring stations in the area to warn of any future attacks. In return, President Sadat permitted Israeli ships to travel through the Suez Canal. Sadat also made an agreement not to launch another attack on Israel.

## Anwar Sadat Stuns the Middle East

President Sadat had won what he considered a major victory. Sadat had established a much stronger relationship with the United States, while bringing peace with Israel. Nevertheless, other Arab nations saw the situation much differently. They believed that he had given in to the Israelis and the powerful American secretary of state, Henry Kissinger. While Sadat regarded Kissinger as "my friend Henry," most other Arab states believed that the United

IN OCTOBER 1974, PLO LEADER YASIR ARAFAT (LEFT) AND EGYPT'S PRESIDENT ANWAR SADAT MET PRIVATELY BEFORE THE OPENING SESSION OF THE ARAB SUMMIT CONFERENCE.

States was little more than Israel's powerful big brother. They believed that the United States was dedicated to keeping the Jews in control of the territory they had conquered in 1967.

Nevertheless, the momentum for change in the Middle East continued. In 1976, a former Democratic governor of Georgia named Jimmy Carter was elected president of the United States. As Carter wrote, "Looking back, it is remarkable to see how constantly the work for peace in the Middle East was on my agenda, and on my mind." Carter had visited the region in the early 1970s, met with Prime Minister Golda Meir, and studied the area extensively. When he became president, Carter was very interested in finding a peaceful solution to Middle East problems.

However, that solution became more difficult in 1977. The Labor Party, led by Prime Minister Yitzhak Rabin, was defeated in the Israeli general elections. Corruption scandals in Rabin's government had turned many voters against the prime minister. In his place, Menachem Begin, leader of the Likud Party, became prime minister of Israel. Begin had a reputation for taking a much stronger position against the Arab states than the Labor leaders. He had criticized the government for agreeing to a ceasefire with Egypt under the Rogers Plan. Begin was also far less willing to compromise over placing new Israeli settlements in the Sinai and West Bank than the Labor leaders had been. He believed that these settlements secured the West Bank for Jews.

Soon after his election Begin traveled to Romania and met with Communist dictator Nicholae Ceausescu. The Romanians, unlike most nations in the Communist world, maintained diplomatic relations with Israel. Soon after Begin's visit, Sadat traveled to Romania. "I asked Ceausescu about his impressions," Sadat wrote. "He said: 'Begin wants a solution.'" Then Sadat asked: "'Can an extremist like Begin really want peace?' 'Let me state categorically to you,' Ceausescu reiterated, 'that he wants peace.'"

Sadat himself said that he was committed to peace.

As Jimmy Carter put it, "Sadat was strong and bold, very much aware of world public opinion and of his role as the most important leader among the Arabs. I always had the impression that he looked on himself as inheriting the mantle of authority from the great pharaohs and was convinced that he was a man of destiny."

On November 7, 1977, President Sadat spoke at a meeting of the Egyptian parliament. In his speech, Sadat stated, "I am ready to go to the end of the world, to their own [Israeli] homes, even to the Knesset [the Israeli Parliament] in search of peace." At first, Sadat's audience was not sure whether he was serious or whether it was just high-sounding words that were part of a political speech. But Sadat was completely serious.

Prime Minister Begin was not sure how to respond to Sadat's speech. But one of Begin's advisors announced the next day that "Sadat would be more than welcome here and would be accorded a proper reception." Shortly afterward, both leaders were interviewed on CBS News—their first joint interview—by anchorman Walter Cronkite. Sadat said that he was waiting for a formal invitation before going to Israel. Begin answered that the Egyptian president would receive the invitation quickly.

On November 19, Sadat flew to Israel to address the Knesset. As he landed at Ben-Gurion Airport, Sadat was greeted by a line of Israeli leaders, including former Prime Minister Golda Meir. "Madame, I have been waiting to meet you for a long time," Sadat said. "And I've waited a long time to meet you," she answered. "Well, the time has arrived, and here I am," Sadat said.

Sadat delivered a strong speech to the Israeli Knesset. While saying, "We welcome you to live among us in peace and security," he also repeated the traditional Arab positions regarding Israel and the Palestinians. These included the statement that the Israelis must give back the lands conquered in the 1967 war. Prime Minister Begin's speech was equally tough.

In their first meeting in Israel, Begin and Sadat did not seem to relate very well to each other. Sadat felt far more comfortable with Defense Minister Ezer Weizman, who seemed more willing to seek a compromise with the Egyptians. But at least it was a start. More meetings were held between Egyptian and Israeli leaders during 1978. Meanwhile, President Carter met separately with Begin and Sadat and other Arab officials. However, there was little progress. The two sides remained too far apart.

Sadat wanted all Israelis out of the Sinai, but Begin refused to give up the Jewish settlements there. The Egyptians also wanted the Israelis to leave the West Bank and grant self-government to the Palestinians. Again, Begin refused to budge. As Sadat put it, "I cannot agree to surrender a single inch of

Arab land. It is sacred." Begin answered him by insisting, "Mr. President, I cannot give up a single inch of [Israel]. It is sacred." The two men were at an impasse.

At this point, Carter decided to invite both men to the United States. He proposed a meeting at the presidential retreat, located at Camp David in the Maryland hills outside of Washington. It was a great risk. If the peace talks failed, then United States prestige in the Middle East would be gravely damaged. In addition, there might be no more peace talks between Sadat and Begin in the near future. As a result, Sadat's trip to Israel would have been a wasted effort. As Carter's National Security Advisor Zbigniew Brzezinski told the president, "It seems to me that if we go public [have talks at Camp David] and then do not prevail, our Middle East policy will be in shambles, and Sadat and others will be either repudiated [by other Arab states] or will turn in a radical direction. In other words, if we go public, we must prevail."

## Meeting at Camp David

The meetings at Camp David began on September 5, 1978. At first Sadat and Begin did little more than repeat their earlier positions. Indeed, the atmosphere between the two men became very heated by the second day. Carter wrote, "All restraint was now gone. Their faces were flushed, and the niceties of diplomatic language and protocol were stripped away. They had almost forgotten that I was there . . ." For the next ten days, the two men refused to meet together face to face. Instead Carter and his advisors walked back and forth between the two different cabins where the Egyptian and Israeli leaders were staying. Carter carried proposals for each man to consider.

As Carter wrote: "I would draft a proposal I considered reasonable, take it to Sadat for quick approval or slight

# The Negotiations That Almost Failed

After more than a week of frustrating negotiations, President Anwar Sadat was about ready to leave Camp David and return to Egypt. As President Jimmy Carter later wrote, "I told Sadat, in effect, that he had betrayed me, had betrayed our friendship, and had violated the commitment he had made that he would give me every opportunity to resolve any differences that arose. . . . I made my statement as strongly as I could. Sadat was taken aback, then told me that he would stay and give me another chance."

Carter used another approach with President Begin to keep him at the meeting. "Begin had asked me to sign some photographs of me, him, and Sadat for his grandchildren," the president wrote. "I got the names of his grandchildren and personalized every photograph. I asked if I could bring the photographs over to his cabin. Begin was still very angry with me, and when I walked into his cabin, there was a frigid atmosphere. I said, 'I've brought you the photographs.' He said, 'Thank you.' I handed him the photographs and, as he looked down, he began calling out the names of his grandchildren. His voice trembled and there were tears running down his cheeks. Then he said, 'We can't leave a war for these little children to fight!'"

modification, and then spend hours or days working on the same point with the Israeli delegation."

Gradually the two sides began to shift and grow closer together. But a major sticking point for Begin were the Jewish settlements in the Sinai Desert. He did not want to give them up. But he was persuaded to accept their removal by a telephone call from Ariel Sharon, who was serving in the Begin government. Sharon had strongly supported the settlements. However, now he "was in favor of evacuating the settlements if they were the last remaining obstacle to a peace agreement."

## Camp David Agreement: Israel, Egypt, and the Palestinians

Finally, by the thirteenth day of the meetings, the three leaders had come up with an agreement. Israel had agreed to give up its airfields and the rest of its military presence in the Sinai. In return, the United States agreed to construct new airfields for Israel in the Negev Desert for defense. Begin was also prepared to remove Israeli settlements from Sinai. As far as the West Bank was concerned, the future remained vague. Begin seemed to say that some local government was possible for the Palestinians, and that the Israelis would not build any new settlements. Sadat thought this meant no new settlements would ever be built. However the Israelis interpreted their statement differently. They believed that new settlements would be stopped for only a short time, and could then continue.

On September 17, 1978, Camp David ended with a preliminary agreement between Israel and Egypt. This included a framework for peace, which called for Israel and the Arabs to discuss eventual self-government for the Palestinians. The agreements also included a peace agreement between Israel and Egypt. It called for the evacuation of the Sinai and diplomatic relations between the two countries.

Both sides still had to iron out the details. This took several more months. Israel finally received assurances that once the Sinai was evacuated, Egypt would not cut off oil supplies from the region. But the issue of autonomy for the Palestinians was never really clarified. Nevertheless, Sadat and Begin signed a final agreement on March 26, 1979.

# Land, the Right of Return, and the Settlements

During the 1980s and 1990s, Israel and the Palestinians continued their decades' old struggles. These revolved around land, the Palestinian right of return, and the Israeli settlements in Gaza and the West Bank. It was a violent struggle, with Israel and the PLO exacting an eye for an eye.

## The Death of Sadat

President Sadat and Prime Minister Begin were hailed in the West for their historic peace agreement. Indeed, both men were awarded the Nobel Peace Prize in 1978. But in the Arab world, attitudes toward the peace agreement were quite different. President Sadat was denounced for abandoning the Palestinian people in order to conclude a treaty with Israel. The Arabs were highly critical of Sadat for establishing diplomatic relations with Israel. As a result, Arab leaders cut off relations with Egypt, expelled Egypt from the Arab League, and refused to deal with President Sadat.

Meanwhile, Sadat continued to negotiate with the Israelis to achieve some type of homeland for the Palestinians. However, President Begin made it clear that he never intended to give the Palestinians anything. As he told Egyptian Prime Minister Mustafa Khalil when he visited Tel Aviv in 1979, "I inform you that Israel will never return to the borders of . . . 1967. . . . Dr. Khalil, a state called Palestine will never be established in Judea, Samaria, and Gaza." So there was no misunderstanding on this point, the Israeli government established new settlements on the West Bank.

Inside Egypt, there was also opposition to the peace agreement. Muslim fundamentalists—radicals who opposed any agreements with the Israelis—denounced Sadat and urged a jihad, or holy war, against the Jews. However, Egypt was a dictatorship that was ruled by President Sadat and his political party. Therefore, Sadat believed that he could ignore the opposition.

On October 6, 1981, Sadat attended a large military celebration near Cairo to commemorate the Egyptian victory in the 1973 war. Sadat, dressed in a brilliant military uniform, reviewed Egyptian military units as they paraded by his reviewing stand. Suddenly, one of the vehicles stopped in front of the president. A man jumped out, followed by other soldiers, and raced toward Sadat. Before the president knew what had happened, he was brutally murdered by automatic gunfire. The assassins were Muslim fundamentalists who hated Sadat. While the West was saddened that a great peacemaker had been killed, Arabs in the Middle East reacted quite differently. They believed that he had sold out to the Israelis. As Sadat's biographers David Hirst and Irene Beeson wrote, "In Syria there was dancing in the streets." In Lebanon, "inhabitants fired into the air. In Libya there were accidents galore as drivers careered about the streets, trumpeting their joy."

# Bloodshed in Lebanon

President Sadat was murdered in Egypt and Arabs cheered. Meanwhile, Israel was gradually being drawn into a bloody battle in Lebanon. Arafat and the PLO had moved their headquarters to Lebanon in the early 1970s, after being expelled from Jordan. Lebanon was sharply divided between Muslims and Arab Christians, who shared political power. The PLO supported the Muslims and began tipping the balance of power in their favor.

Supplied with money and weapons by other Arab states, Arafat established his own political power base in Lebanon. The PLO won the support of many Palestinians, who had been living in the Lebanese refugee camps since the 1948 war. The PLO set up hospitals and schools and provided jobs for many poor refugees. From bases inside the refugee camps, the PLO also launched attacks on central Israel, as well as on Israeli settlements in Gaza and the West Bank. Barry and Judith Rubin point out that the PLO leader not only wanted to recapture Gaza and the West Bank but to destroy the entire state of Israel.

Meanwhile, the PLO army worked with the Muslims to defeat the Christian forces and take over Lebanon. However, Syria, Lebanon's eastern neighbor, did not want the Lebanese state to fall into PLO hands. Syrian President Hafez Assad wanted to control Lebanon himself. Assad demanded that Arafat stop fighting for control of Lebanon. "You do not represent the Palestinians more than we do," Assad angrily told Arafat. "Don't you forget. . . . There is no Palestinian people and there is no Palestinian entity [state]. There is [only] Syria." But Arafat paid no attention to him. Not only did he continue the civil war in Lebanon, but the PLO also attacked settlements southward in Israel. This prompted retaliation from the Israeli army, turning southern Lebanon into a bloody battleground: 50,000 Lebanese were killed and 100,000 wounded.

Finally, in 1976, Syria invaded Lebanon. Assad stated that he had entered the country to bring peace between Muslims and Christians. In reality, he had decided to occupy a large area in the eastern part of the country, known as the Bekaa Valley, and take over the Lebanese capital, Beirut. This gave the Syrians control of most of the country. The PLO was only permitted to operate in southern Lebanon, where it continued to launch attacks against Israel. By the early 1980s, PLO troops were launching missiles on Israeli settlements in Galilee, threatening the lives of thousands of settlers. Israel struck back with attacks on PLO positions. The Israeli government also supplied arms to the Christian forces in Lebanon who were battling the PLO.

On June 3, 1982, the Israeli ambassador to England was nearly assassinated. Although the PLO probably had nothing to do with the assassination attempt, Prime Minister Begin believed that the time had come to retaliate. On June 6, Begin ordered operation Peace for Galilee to begin in Lebanon. Following the advice of Defense Minister Ariel Sharon, Begin had decided that the IDF should advance 20 miles (40 kilometers) into southern Lebanon. Begin wanted to clear out the PLO and take their missiles out of range of the Galilean settlements. However, Sharon may have intended something far different than what he told Begin. Some historians believe that Sharon really intended to establish a foothold in southern Lebanon, and expand it until he had reached Beirut—the headquarters of the PLO. And Begin may have known this all along.

However, the Israeli cabinet was told nothing. "Mr. Defense Minister," Begin said to Sharon in a cabinet meeting, "would you be kind enough to explain the military plan to the cabinet." Sharon later wrote, "I presented the operation. I explained what the targets were, and that the aim was to hit the PLO in Lebanon." When asked about Beirut, Sharon said, "Beirut is out of the picture. This operation is not designed to capture Beirut, but to create a forty-to-forty-five-kilometer area in which there will no longer be any terrorists."

The IDF easily advanced northward and approached Beirut, beginning a nine-week siege of the capital. Arafat was holed up inside the capital, defended by PLO fighters. At this point, Western governments intervened to give Arafat an escape route. Sharon knew that advancing into Beirut and destroying the PLO was not in the original plan presented to the cabinet and the Israeli people. Therefore, he accepted the help of the U.S. government, which offered to transfer Arafat and the PLO out of Lebanon. In late August 1982, they were taken to Tunis, the capital of Tunisia, located in North Africa.

In September, Lebanese Christian military units were permitted by the Israelis to march into the Palestinian refugee camps of Sabra and Shatila in Beirut. Their mission was to root out PLO militia who were suspected of still living in the refugee camps. Instead, the Christian militia began to massacre innocent Palestinian refugees, and about one thousand were killed. As a result of the massacre, Sharon was forced to resign as defense minister. In 1983, Begin resigned as prime minister.

The IDF gradually retreated from Beirut to a defensive position in southern Lebanon. Meanwhile, the Syrians remained in Lebanon and took control of much of the country. They continued to dominate Lebanon until their 2005 withdrawal from the country.

## Eye for an Eye

From its new headquarters in Tunis, the PLO continued to launch violent attacks against its enemies. In 1983, the PLO may have been involved in attacks on the U.S. embassy in Lebanon, in which sixty-three Americans were killed. PLO terrorists also led an attack on the U.S. Marine base in Beirut, which led to the death of 241 soldiers.

ISRAELIS DEMONSTRATE OUTSIDE OF PRIME MINISTER MENACHEM BEGIN'S HOME IN PROTEST AGAINST THE MASSACRE OF ARABS IN SABRA-SHATILLA, LEBANON, IN 1982.

Meanwhile, some PLO units returned to Lebanon and attacked Israeli settlements.

In May 1985, the PLO set off a series of bombs in Jerusalem. On September 25, PLO terrorists murdered three Israeli civilians visiting the Mediterranean island nation of Cyprus. Less than a week later, on October 1, the Israeli air force struck the PLO headquarters in Tunis, killing around sixty of its officials. The IDF also destroyed the homes of suspected PLO members, destroyed farms, imprisoned Palestinian officials, and even carried out assassinations of PLO leaders. Finally, near the end of the year, PLO agents hijacked a cruise ship, the *Achille Lauro*. The agents murdered one of the passengers, a Jewish tourist. The terrorists were eventually rounded up by a U.S. rescue squad after they tried to escape. Passengers aboard the ship later said that the terrorists had proclaimed, "We came on behalf of Yasir Arafat."

## The Long Road to Peace

While bloody clashes were occurring in the Middle East, peace efforts were under way behind the scenes. During the mid–1980s, the Likud and Labor parties had been sharing power. Neither party had been able to win a majority of votes in the Knesset. Likud leader Yitzhak Shamir served as prime minister, while Labor leader Shimon Peres held the office of foreign minister. Donning an elaborate disguise, Peres journeyed to London in 1987 for a secret meeting with Jordan's King Hussein. Hussein had maintained secret contacts with Israel for many years.

Although the Israelis refused to deal with the PLO, Peres and Hussein agreed that Israel would negotiate with a delegation that included Jordanians and Palestinians living on the West Bank. However, Israel insisted that these Palestinians had to accept U.N. Resolutions 242 and 338. These resolutions guaranteed the right of Israel to exist as a state. The PLO, on the other hand, had dedicated itself to destroying the state of Israel.

After reaching an agreement, Peres returned to Israel to talk with Shamir. The prime minister refused to go along with the deal. "It was always Peres's position that we must make an agreement with King Hussein . . . and give up a large piece of Judea and Samaria [the West Bank] to make peace. I was against it."

## The Settlements and the Intifada

Meanwhile, Palestinians living on the West Bank had grown impatient with the Israeli presence there. They looked around them and saw an increasing number of Jewish settlers on the West Bank and continuing occupation by Israeli soldiers. In December 1987, a military vehicle carrying Israelis had struck a car, killing four

Palestinians. At the funeral that followed, thousands of Palestinians gathered to express their sadness as well as their anger at the Israelis. Although the IDF tried to keep tension under control, Palestinians began throwing stones at the soldiers. One of the soldiers fired and killed a seventeen-year-old boy. Israelis said this was an accident, but Palestinians disagreed, believing it was deliberate.

Suddenly, Palestinian outrage at the Israelis broke out across the West Bank and Gaza Strip in a series of riots. At first the Israeli government thought that the uprising would come and go quickly. But it spread, led by young Palestinians who wanted to express their opposition to Israeli rule. Known as an Intifada, the uprising occurred without any planning or overall direction. In Tunis, Yasir Arafat and the other PLO leaders quickly realized that they might be pushed to the sidelines by new, younger Palestinian leaders in Gaza and the West Bank.

The West Bank settlements of the Palestinians felt like occupied territory. The IDF had set up roadblocks restricting Palestinian travel. As a result, Palestinians had difficulty traveling from their homes to their jobs each day. Palestinian communities were separated from each other by Israeli settlements, making communications between Arabs very difficult.

Nevertheless, PLO agents still lived on the West Bank. Under the leadership of Abu Jihad, a close associate of Yasir Arafat, the PLO gradually began to assert control over the Intifada. Early in 1988, the Israeli government struck back at the PLO. Israeli agents were sent to Tunis, where they murdered Abu Jihad at his villa on the Mediterranean. Arafat realized that he had to take new steps in order to guarantee the future leadership of the PLO over the Intifada. In November 1988, he announced at a meeting of the Palestinian National Council that he supported U.N. resolutions 242 and 338.

The United States had refused to talk to Arafat until he recognized the right of Israel to exist as a state. Arafat hoped that by taking this step, the United States would pressure Israel to open negotiations for a Palestinian state.

But the United States was still not convinced that Arafat had gone far enough. George Schultz, U.S. secretary of state in the Reagan administration, had been pressuring Arafat to agree to give up violence and terrorism. In December 1988, Arafat finally took this step. At a press conference, Arafat announced, "The executive committee of the PLO, I repeat for the record, totally and absolutely renounces all forms of tourism . . . Sorry, I meant terrorism," he joked.

## Peace Talks in Madrid

Relations between Israel and the PLO did not occur in a vacuum. That is, they were influenced by the United States, as well as by other Arab nations, such as Jordan and Egypt. In August 1990, Iraq, an Arab state, invaded its neighbor Kuwait. Iraqi leader Saddam Hussein seized control of the rich Kuwaiti oil fields. U.S. President George H.W. Bush announced that the Iraqi leader would not be allowed to remain in Kuwait. Bush rapidly put together a large coalition opposing Iraq that included most Arab nations in the Middle East. Bush even persuaded Hafez Assad, an old enemy of the United States, to join the coalition. Bush promised, "Once we are done dealing with Saddam, once we are done liberating Kuwait, you have my word that the United States will turn to the peace process, and will turn to it in a determined, fair way."

Meanwhile, the Iraqi leader said that he would leave Kuwait if, in return, the Israelis promised to evacuate the West Bank. Saddam's statement won the support of many Palestinians. The PLO became one of the only groups in the Middle East to back Iraq. Once Iraq was defeated early in 1991, Arafat and the PLO leadership found themselves in a very weak position because of their support of Saddam Hussein.

Following the end of the war in Kuwait, President Bush sent Secretary of State James Baker to the Middle East. Baker's mission was to jump-start the peace process between Israel, the Palestinians, and the other Arab states. Baker refused to deal with the PLO, which had backed Saddam Hussein. Instead he agreed to deal with a joint Jordanian and Palestinian delegation from the West Bank. As part of his mission to the Middle East, Baker also talked to Hafez Assad in Syria. In the past, the Syrians had received military support from the Soviet Union. But by the 1990s, the Soviet Union was breaking up into independent states and no longer had the economic power to assist its former allies. As a result, Assad was more willing to support peace efforts. Finally, Baker convinced Israeli Prime Minister Shamir to have face-to-face talks with the Palestinians. However, Shamir was still unwilling to give up any territory on the West Bank.

On October 31, 1991, Arab and Israeli delegations met together in Madrid, Spain. The brief conference lasted only three days. Nevertheless, it marked the first time that all sides in the Palestinian dispute had gathered together for talks. The discussions continued in Moscow and later Washington. However, the delegations found themselves far apart on many important issues.

## The Oslo Accords

In 1992, the Israeli Labor Party, led by Yitzhak Rabin, won a major election victory. Rabin became the new prime minister, promising to achieve a peace treaty with the Palestinians on the West Bank within a year. Nevertheless, talks were stalled in Washington, and no agree-

**PRESIDENT BILL CLINTON BRINGS ISRAELI PRIME MINISTER YITZHAK RABIN (L) AND PLO CHAIRMAN YASIR ARAFAT TOGETHER FOR A HISTORIC HANDSHAKE AFTER THE SIGNING OF THE ISRAELI-PLO PEACE ACCORD AT THE WHITE HOUSE ON SEPTEMBER 13, 1993.**

ment looked possible. Behind the scenes, however, another set of discussions were under way. With the blessing of Rabin and Arafat, Israeli and PLO negotiators were meeting in Oslo, Norway. Arafat needed to show progress in establishing a Palestinian state to retain his position as leader of the Palestinians.

The talks continued throughout much of 1993, almost breaking apart at one point, but finally reaching an agreement. On September 13, 1993, Arafat and Rabin met at the White House in Washington, D.C. The meeting was held there to emphasize U.S. support for the agreement. In front of U.S. President Bill Clinton, the men shook hands with each other, after they were privately persuaded to do so by the president. According to the terms of the agreement, known as Oslo I, the PLO recognized the right of Israel to exist as a state and renounced the use of terrorism. In return, Prime Minister Rabin agreed "to recognize the PLO as the representative of the Palestinian people and will commence negotiations with the PLO within the Middle East peace process."

These negotiations continued over the next two years, leading to another peace agreement, known as Oslo II, in 1995. Under the terms of this agreement, the PLO took over more than half of Gaza and about 4 percent of the territory on the West Bank. This included several West Bank towns, such as Bethlehem, Jericho, and Nablus. Over the next five years, more territory was expected to be transferred to the Palestinians. Meanwhile, Israel established diplomatic relations with Jordan. Peace for Israel and a Palestinian homeland seemed a giant step closer than ever before.

## Politics and Violence

The Oslo peace process called for a new government in the Palestinian lands. Known as the Palestinian Authority (PA), the government held its first elections on January 20, 1996. Yasir Arafat was elected president of the PA, and a majority of his supporters won election to the new Palestinian parliament. In the new government, most power remained in the hands of Arafat. However, he proved to be a better guerrilla leader than president of a new government. The PA had to create a government administration, establish economic policies, build a police force, and set up a legal system. Arafat had no experience in any of these areas. The new government experienced serious economic problems. Governments in Europe contributed several billion

# What Does It Mean to Be Israeli?

The majority of Israeli citizens are Jews—over 80 percent—but more than 15 percent are Arab. Many Israelis came from Western Europe after World War II, but Jewish immigrants have also come more recently from Russia, where they were persecuted by the Soviet regime. Other immigrants left other areas of the Middle East, Africa, and the United States to settle in Israel—for various reasons.

Hebrew is the official language of Israel, but Muslims speak Arabic and Israelis often communicate in English. While many Israelis are Orthodox, which means they have strong religious beliefs and obey strict religious rules, many other Israelis are not religious at all, but maintain a cultural link to the Jewish faith and history. The Israeli state is, however, a religious state, which means that whether or not a citizen is Jewish or religious, he or she must follow religious rules. For example, business as usual stops on the Sabbath—Friday at sundown until Saturday at sundown—for everyone. If you want to shop, eat out, or use public transportation in Israel on the Sabbath, for example, you are out of luck.

dollars to the PA. But much of the money went to building up a Palestinian police force rather than trying to improve agriculture in the Palestinian territory. Large amounts of aid were also mismanaged by corrupt PA officials. Arab states gave very little money to the PA. While these states had publicly supported a Palestinian homeland, they did not support Arafat. Arab states feared that most of their money would be stolen by his corrupt officials.

Jobs were difficult for the Palestinians to find. Thousands had been employed in Kuwait, working in the oilfields. However, the Palestinians supported the invasion of Kuwait by Saddam Hussein. As a result, they were expelled following the Iraqi defeat in the Gulf War. Many Palestinians had to depend on the PA to find them jobs in the police force or other government departments. Other Palestinians had traveled to Israel to work.

Violence broke out after the signing of the Oslo accords. Radical Palestinian groups, such as Hamas and the Popular Front for the Liberation of Palestine (PFLP), set off bombs in Israel, killing innocent citizens. As a result, Israel began closing its borders to Palestinians, preventing them from coming into the country to work. Palestinians working in Israel dropped from 120,000 in 1993 to 30,000 in 1995. Although Arafat criticized the violence, he seemed unwilling to stop the activities of the radical groups. Perhaps he believed that violence would persuade the Israelis to give up more territory to the PA. Arafat may have also feared that supporters of Hamas might try to undermine his government.

Meanwhile, Israeli Prime Minister Yitzhak Rabin was also being criticized by political opponents who believed that he had given away too much to the Palestinians. In November 1995, Rabin attended a peace rally in Tel Aviv. After leaving the rally, Rabin was approached by Yigal Amir, a radical opposed to the peace process. Amir pulled out a gun and shot Rabin. The prime minister died as he was being rushed to a nearby hospital. Rabin's funeral in Jerusalem was attended by many world leaders, including Jordan's King Hussein, who spoke at the ceremony. "I never thought that a moment such as this would come," Hussein said, "when I would grieve the loss of a brother, a colleague, and a friend . . . I realized, as he did, that we have to cross over the divide, establish a dialogue, get to know each other and strive to leave for those who follow us a legacy that is worthy of them."

After Rabin's death, foreign minister Shimon Peres became prime minister. But the Labor government seemed unable to stop the violent attacks by Palestinian radical groups inside Israel. As a result, Labor was defeated by the Likud Party in the 1996 election. The new prime minister, Benjamin Netanyahu, promised to be tougher in dealing with the Palestinians. Netanyahu had not supported the Oslo peace process and did not want to continue dealing with Arafat.

Nevertheless, Netanyahu faced tremendous pressure from the United States to continue the efforts begun at Oslo. In January 1997, Israel turned over most of the city of Hebron on the West Bank to the Palestinian Authority. This transfer had been expected as part of the Oslo accords.

## Wye Agreements

Nevertheless, the PLO attacks combined with Netanyahu's opposition to Oslo meant that the peace process was slowing down. President Bill Clinton tried to keep the process going with a meeting in October 1998. Arafat, Netanyahu, and Clinton held peace talks at Wye Plantation in Maryland. Since Arafat and Netanyahu did not want to deal with each other, the discussions reached a deadlock. King

Hussein was visiting the United States for cancer treatment while the Wye discussions were occurring. Although the king was extremely sick and would die shortly afterward, he traveled to Wye. In a statement at Wye, King Hussein urged the participants to reach an agreement. "There has been enough destruction, enough death, enough waste," he said. Shortly afterward, the two sides reached an agreement. Under its terms, Israel promised to turn over more territory to the PA on the West Bank. Israel also agreed to permit the PA to build an airport and seaport in Gaza, and allow Palestinians to travel freely between Gaza and the West Bank.

Shortly after Wye, however, Arafat said that the peace process had not gone far enough. He had expected that Oslo would lead to the establishment of a Palestinian state. Arafat stated that if this did not happen, the PA would declare a Palestinian state in 1999 with Jerusalem as its capital. "The Palestinian rifle is ready and we will aim it if they try to prevent us from praying in Jerusalem," he announced in November 1998.

KING HUSSEIN OF JORDAN KEPT UP SECRET CONTACTS IN ISRAEL FOR MANY YEARS. IN 1998, THOUGH FATALLY ILL, HE TRAVELED TO THE WYE PLANTATION IN MARYLAND TO URGE THE PARTICIPANTS IN THE PEACE TALKS TO MAKE AN AGREEMENT.

## Back to Camp David

Many Israelis were eager for peace and an end to terrorism. In 1999, they elected a new prime minister, Ehud Barak. Barak was prepared to go much further than Netanyahu to reach an agreement with Arafat. In spring 2000, meetings were held between Israeli and Palestinian negotiators, leading to a final discussion between Barak and Arafat at Camp David with President Clinton.

At the meetings, Israeli and Palestinian negotiators discussed various issues, such as the size of a new Palestinian state, the right of Palestinian refugees to return to Israel, and the final status of Jerusalem. Prime Minister Barak agreed to hand over all of Gaza to the PA, as well as more than 90 percent of the West Bank and the Palestinian neighborhoods in East Jerusalem. In Jerusalem, the PA would establish their new capital. In addition, Jews and Palestinians would share control of the Temple Mount containing the Jewish Temple and the Dome of the Rock. No Israeli prime minister had offered so much.

But it was not enough for Arafat, who rejected the offer. President Clinton was furious. "If the Israelis can make compromises and you can't, I should go home. . . . These things have consequences; failure will mean the end of the peace process," Clinton told him. But Arafat kept demanding all of East Jerusalem, all of Gaza and the West Bank, and the right of all Palestinian refugees to go back to Israel.

Why the disconnect between the two sides? Historian Cheryl Rubenberg emphasized that Arafat and the Palestinians did not trust Israel and the United States. Although President Clinton had invited Arafat to the White House on several occasions, Clinton had never discussed the possibility of a Palestinian state with the PA leader. In the meantime, the United States did nothing to pressure Israel to stop building new settlements on the West Bank. These settlements indicated to the Palestinians that Israel would never return to its pre–1967 war borders and give Arafat the Palestinian state that he wanted. In addition, the United States gave billions of dollars in aid to Israel, regarding the Israelis as a principal ally in the Middle East.

Rubenberg argued that a myth came out of Camp David that Barak had made a "generous" offer and Arafat had rejected it because of his "intransigence." But the offer stated that most Israeli settlers would remain on the West Bank. As a result, Palestinian communities would be separated from each other by "checkpoints, roadblocks, and permits" necessary to travel from one place to another around the Israeli settlements. Thus, the new Palestinian state would not be unified, but include separate sections. These would consist of Gaza; Jericho; a northern section with towns such as Nablus and Jenin; a central section including Ramallah; and a southern section. In Jerusalem, Israelis lived in each Palestinian neighborhood. So, Barak's proposal to give the PA control of the Palestinian sections had little value. Finally, Barak refused to discuss any concrete proposals for the refugee issue. As Rubenberg put it, "not a position Arafat could have presented to his people. The prime minister [Barak] did make very clear, however, that there could be no right of return."

According to historian Efraim Karsh, the Israelis saw the Camp David summit as a chance for negotiations, but Arafat did not intend to give up any of his demands. "In stark contrast to Israeli counterparts, Arafat had never viewed the negotiations as a give-and-take process in which both sides were supposed to make painful concessions and meet somewhere in between, but rather as a redress of an historical wrong in which Israel was to give the Palestinians what was rightfully theirs without getting anything meaningful in return." As Arafat himself put it, "If anyone thinks that I can sign away Jerusalem, he is deluding himself. . . . We told the Israelis," he said later to a large crowd in Gaza, that "we demand the whole of Jerusalem, the whole of Jerusalem."

Historian Anton LaGuardia believed that Arafat was fearful of Palestinian public opinion. Many had criticized Arafat for not demanding more at Oslo. Now Arafat feared that anything less than the demands he had made for years would be a "surrender" to Israel and the United States.

So, another possible opportunity for peace was lost. Once again an agreement had been impossible because of the settlement issue, the Palestinian right of return, and control of land—the future of Jerusalem. The level of violence increased as a new Intifada broke out on the West Bank and in Gaza.

# Opposing Political Leaders

For years, Israeli and Palestinian political leaders faced each other across battlefields in the Middle East. The PLO was led by Yasir Arafat until his death in 2004. The Israeli leaders included Menachem Begin, Yitzhak Rabin, and Shimon Peres. But perhaps no two men exemplified the Palestinian-Israeli conflict better than Arafat and Ariel Sharon.

## The New Intifada

In September 2000, Ariel Sharon visited the Dome of the Rock in Jerusalem. A retired general and leader of the Likud Party, Sharon was accompanied by members of his political party as well as 1,200 police for protection. Palestinians in East Jerusalem viewed Sharon as a harsh opponent of their desires for a homeland and did not want him to visit their sacred religious site. The Israeli government feared for his safety. Palestinian protestors threw rocks at the police when Sharon visited. A day later, the demonstrations increased, with more people hurling rocks at the police. The armed Israeli police began firing at the crowd, injuring two hundred and killing four demonstrators. The demonstrations quickly spread from Jerusalem to Palestinian towns along the West Bank and in Gaza. Over one hundred people died by the end of the month. The Al-Aqsa Intifada—named after one of the mosques at the Dome of the Rock—had begun.

The Intifada arose for several reasons. Palestinians were frustrated with Israel because they had not received a homeland after the long negotiations. Palestinians resented their living conditions on the West Bank and in Gaza, which was heavily restricted by the roadblocks and permits they needed to travel from one area to the other. As a result, it took much longer for Palestinians to reach their jobs, for their children to attend school, and for the sick to receive medical care. Many Palestinians blamed the United States, in part, for this situation because it gave strong support to Israel. The Palestinians were also angry with Arafat and his officials for running a corrupt government and not achieving the homeland that they had promised.

Jewish historian Efraim Karsh sees other reasons for the Intifada. After the clashes at the Temple Mount, Arafat immediately accused Israel of "exacting a painful revenge on the Palestinians for their courage and steadfastness." Arafat tried to portray the visit of Sharon and the response by Israeli police as a calculated attack on the Palestinians. As he told a meeting of the Arab League late in 2000, "Most of the Israeli political and military leaders admitted that they had been planning for more than a year to ignite this fire." But, according to Karsh, the Intifada was "a deliberate attempt by Arafat to force Israel to top [increase] its Camp David proposals without receiving anything in return." Arafat urged his supporters to respond to Sharon's visit with rocks and demonstrations. This was Arafat's attempt to gain support from Palestinians and various Arab countries, after turning down the deal at Camp David. He had used violence in the past to pressure Israel, Karsh said, so he decided to use it again. Karsh was only partly right.

Arafat also represented the frustrations of the Palestinian people who felt that the Oslo agreements did not give them what they had been promised. While Arafat may have helped begin the new Intifada, he did not control it. The new Intifada included members of a variety of Palestinian groups, such as Islamic Jihad, the Al-Aqsa Martyrs Brigade, and Hamas. Many of the demonstrators were also young men and women who operated on their own. Once the Intifada had begun, however, Arafat seemed to do little to stop it. According to a U.S. official, "He was not going to stand in the way of the tiger, so he rode it."

Meanwhile, Prime Minister Barak was unable to put down the Intifada. He had also failed to bring peace to Israel. In elections held during 2001, the Israeli people turned to Ariel Sharon, who became the new prime minister. Sharon promised to break the Intifada with force. Once this was done, he envisioned giving the Palestinians a small homeland in part of Gaza and the West Bank. Palestinian towns would be separated from each other by Israeli settlements and the IDF. As a result, no strong, unified Palestinian state would ever be permitted to exist.

## Violence Begets Violence

Sharon and Arafat were locked in a violent showdown for the future of Israel and the Palestinian state. Sharon had long supported building settlements in Gaza and the West Bank. He regarded these settlements as well as the presence of the IDF as a strong defense against an invasion of central Israel. From 1993 to 2000, there was more than a 50 percent increase in the number of homes built by Israeli settlers on the West Bank and in Gaza. The settler population grew from 115,000 in 1993 to 200,000 in 2000.

Major targets of the Intifada were the Israeli settlers in and around East Jerusalem as well as along the West Bank and in Gaza. During the 1990s, about 60 percent of the Palestinians supported the Oslo peace plan. But as more and more Israeli settlements were built on the West Bank, Palestinian support for the peace process declined. Support had reached 11 percent by 2001. Shortly after Ariel Sharon's election, battles erupted in Gaza between the IDF and Palestinians.

The IDF later took control of part of Gaza, which had been under the direction of the PA. According to the Israeli government, this action was aimed at stopping Palestinians from firing artillery into Jewish settlements near Gaza.

In March, the Israeli government tried to cut off the Palestinian towns of Ramallah and Jericho from the rest of the West Bank. Sharon hoped that by isolating Palestinians he could prevent terrorist attacks in central Israel. Some of these attacks were made by young Palestinian suicide bombers. They were deeply distressed over the plight of the Palestinians on the West Bank and in Gaza. Many believed that the only way to stop Israel was to take revenge on Israeli citizens. They had seen homes and farms destroyed by the Israelis, and many of their friends imprisoned by the IDF. Out of despair, the suicide bombers were ready to sacrifice themselves as well as the lives of innocent Israelis.

In May 2001, suicide bombers struck an Israeli shopping mall, killing six people. Other suicide bombers struck a dance club in Tel Aviv, killing twenty-one Israelis and injuring about another one hundred people.

Meanwhile, the United States was trying to convince Israel and the Palestinians to put an end to the violence and return to the negotiating table. Under the direction of President George W. Bush, the United States submitted a new peace plan. It was negotiated by Central Intelligence Agency Director George Tenet. Under the terms of the Tenet document, both sides agreed to a ceasefire. Israelis also agreed to withdraw from areas newly occupied by the IDF in return for the PA arresting Palestinians planning to launch attacks against Israel.

But there was no end to the violence. Palestinians in the West Bank town of Beit Jala fired on Israelis living in nearby Jerusalem, prompting the IDF to march against Beit Jala. In November, the Israeli government assassinated Mahmoud Abu Hanoud, a Hamas leader, who had directed many of the terrorist attacks. But the following month a Hamas suicide bomber struck Jerusalem, killing eleven people. Another Hamas bomber struck Haifa, killing fifteen Israelis.

Sharon blamed Arafat for not putting an end to the violence and ordered the bombing of PA government buildings in Gaza and the West Bank. Arafat may have been unwilling or unable to stop the acts of terrorists, but Sharon also seemed to believe that violence was the only way to stop the Palestinians. As Alexander Cockburn, an anti-Israeli columnist, wrote in the *Nation*, "In the wake of the recent suicide bomb attacks launched by Hamas, the sky is now the limit for Israeli reprisals: the killing of Arafat, and not so far down the road, perhaps forced expulsion of tens of thousands of Palestinians from the West Bank."

## The Violence Continues

On September 11, 2001, the United States was struck by al-Qaeda terrorist attacks. Suddenly American citizens found themselves on the front lines of terrorism. The 9/11 bombings strengthened the relationship between Israel and the United States, who seemed to be joined as allies in the struggle against terrorism. The administration of George W. Bush supported Sharon when he launched Operation Journey of Colors in February 2002. Prime Minister Sharon sent in the IDF to take control of most Palestinian towns on the West Bank and in Gaza. The IDF was hunting suspected Palestinian terrorists. As Palestinians were rounded up and arrested, the IDF destroyed homes and hospitals in many towns. After this brief assault, the IDF withdrew. But the assault was followed by a new wave of Palestinian suicide bombings.

In March, Sharon ordered another attack by the IDF—Operation Defensive Shield. The army invaded Gaza and the West Bank once again. This time the Palestinians were forced to remain inside their homes, while Israeli soldiers patrolled the streets. Clashes between the IDF and Palestinians led to many deaths. Again, the Israeli attack was followed by Palestinian suicide bombings launched by Hamas. This led to another IDF attack—Operation Determined Path—in June and July of 2002. This time, the IDF took complete control of the Palestinian towns on the West Bank.

Yasir Arafat was forced to remain at PA headquarters in Ramallah. A virtual prisoner in his government compound, he was powerless to stop the IDF. Prime Minister Sharon talked openly about replacing Arafat with force, and continued to bomb his government buildings. "Pray for me to attain martyrdom," Arafat said. "Is there anything better than being martyred on this holy land?" But Sharon stopped short of killing the Palestinian leader.

## Building the Wall

Meanwhile Prime Minister Sharon had begun a new approach to reducing terrorism. The Israeli government began building a fence along the Green Line—the pre–1967 war borders of Israel. Most of the suicide bombers infiltrated central Israel from the West Bank across the Green Line. A fence was erected between Israel and the Gaza Strip during the 1990s, which prevented suicide bombers from crossing into Israel from Gaza.

While the fence was being started, suicide bombings continued. Israel struck back in July, assassinating Hamas military leader Salah Shehada. An Israeli jet dropped a

**TO DEFEND ITSELF AGAINST PALESTINIAN SUICIDE BOMBERS, THE ISRAELI GOVERNMENT DECIDED TO BUILD A FENCE ALONG THE GREEN LINE. WHO BUILT THE FENCE? PALESTINIAN LABORERS.**

bomb on his apartment building in Gaza City. The bomb killed Shehada as well as 13 other Palestinians and wounded another 145, including children.

By the end of 2002, 700 Israelis and more than 2,000 Palestinians had been killed. Early in 2003, Prime Minister Sharon was reelected by the Israeli people, a majority of whom believed that he was the best leader to deal with security issues. The defensive wall continued to be built by Israelis to protect themselves from suicide bombers. In some cases, the wall ran right through towns such as Bethlehem on the West Bank. Claire Anastas, a Palestinian, found that she and her children would be living on one side of the wall, separated from most of their friends on the other side. The wall was being put in this location to protect Jews who wanted to visit an important religious shrine.

## No Peace in Sight

Nevertheless, the Palestinian attacks continued during 2003. Hamas launched suicide bombing attacks and shelled Israeli towns across the border from Gaza. The IDF

DESPITE ISRAELI ACTIONS, THE PALESTINIAN GROUP, HAMAS, CONTINUED ITS ATTACKS AGAINST ISRAEL. HERE, A HAMAS MILITANT MARCHES HOLDING A KORAN DURING A RALLY AT THE RAFAH REFUGEE CAMP IN GAZA IN SUPPORT OF IRAQ. IRAQ HAD PAID AT LEAST $30 MILLION TO SUPPORT THE FAMILIES OF PALESTINIANS KILLED IN THE INTIFADA.

struck back, raiding Palestinian refugee camps and towns. They also continued to occupy northern Gaza. In April, a new peace plan, known as the Road Map, was proposed by leaders from the United States, the United Nations, Europe, and Russia. Under the plan, the Palestinians were expected to put an end to violence leading to a peace agreement that would include a Palestinian state by 2005. However, the Sharon government refused to negotiate with Arafat, whom Sharon held responsible for the violence.

Meanwhile, the United States had also decided that Arafat could not be trusted to negotiate a peace agreement. President Bush had called Arafat "the main obstacle" to peace. In 2003, the Palestinian legislature selected a new prime minister, Mahmoud Abbas, also known as Abu Mazen. A longtime associate of Arafat's, Abbas was involved in negotiating the Oslo peace agreements during the 1990s.

After the announcement of the Road Map, however, little progress was made. In late August, the IDF attacked a laboratory in Nablus on the West Bank where Hamas made explosives. Palestinian suicide bombings began again. The Israeli government retaliated with the assassination of Mohammed Sidr, an Islamic Jihad leader. Abbas did not have the power to stop the suicide attacks and he was "constantly undercut by . . . Arafat," according to *Time* magazine. During the fall, Abbas resigned.

Early in 2004, the IDF attacked radical Palestinians linked to Hamas in Gaza City, killing fifteen of them and wounding forty. This may have been a calculated policy by Sharon. The prime minister had announced that he planned to pull out of Gaza. This meant that all Israeli settlements there would be dismantled and the settlers forced to leave. However, Sharon wanted to show the Palestinian radicals that he still meant to deal with them harshly.

Battles continued in Gaza. Meanwhile, Israelis also continued building their massive security fence, which would stretch for about four hundred miles. Observation posts were being built at intervals along the fence to provide extra defense against possible Palestinian attacks. Many Israelis supported the building of the fence. Nahum and Dalia Atar are a Jewish couple who live near the fence on the West Bank. Together with their five sons, they run a farm that grows lemons. "As tension grew," said Dotan Atar, one of Nahum's sons, "it got less and less safe for us here. . . . One farmer was stabbed to death while in his fields. We even forbid our father to go out there alone. Now that is all over. The fence means security."

## The Road to Peace

The West Bank and Gaza may form two very different elements of the Israeli peace plan. Sharon was preparing to leave Gaza. Indeed, President Bush praised Sharon for his intention to hand Gaza over to the Palestinians. But Palestinians feared that while they might receive Gaza, they would get little else from Sharon. Sharon "seemed to want to create a [small] state in Gaza and that's all," according to historian Salim Tamari.

Palestinians continued to demand a return to the pre–1967 boundaries. Yet as the *Economist* pointed out, "neither demand is taken seriously by serious peacemakers, including by the Palestinians themselves." During the negotiations with President Clinton in 2000, the Palestinians were prepared to let Israel keep some of the larger settlements on the West Bank in exchange for land elsewhere. The *Economist* added that Gaza "is probably the best that can be achieved for as long as the intifada rages."

Other observers, however, pointed out that even Gaza will not be under complete Palestinian control. Phyllis Bennis, a member of the Institute for Policy Studies, wrote that even if Israel left Gaza, Palestinian leaders would not be in charge of the area. The Israeli air force would still dominate the air routes over Gaza. The coastline would be patrolled by Israeli naval ships. In addition, Bennis added that the fence would leave the West Bank permanently divided between an Israeli and Palestinian section. Thus the Palestinians on the West Bank would be cut off from those in Gaza.

The peace plan did not bring an end to violence. Clashes continued in Gaza between Hamas and the IDF. By the end of 2004, more than 2,800 Palestinians and 1,000 Israelis had died. While many Israelis supported Sharon's peace initiative, others believed that he was simply giving in to violence. They denounced him for pulling out of Gaza. Nevertheless, only about 8,000 settlers in Gaza would be affected by the pull-out. In October, the Israeli Knesset, in a close vote, backed Sharon's plan.

# After Arafat and Sharon

Meanwhile, Arafat's health had suddenly begun to decline. Arafat had been forced to remain in PA headquarters in Ramallah, where he was surrounded by the IDF. But as the seventy-five-year-old Arafat's health grew worse, the Israeli government permitted him to be flown to Paris, France, for treatment, guaranteeing that he could return to Ramallah when his health improved. Arafat did not return, dying in Paris on November 11, 2004. Palestinian leaders immediately selected Mahmoud Abbas to replace him.

Does the passing of Arafat break the deadlock between the Palestinian leader and Sharon that has existed for so many years? Abbas is considered far more moderate than Arafat, and is known to oppose the Intifada. Elected prime minister by the Palestinian people in January 2005, Abbas began clamping down on Hamas and other radical groups. In February, he fired several of his security officials for not preventing Palestinian radicals from attacking Israeli settlements in Gaza. In response, the government of Prime Minister Sharon announced that it would cease destroying the homes of the families of suicide bombers on the West Bank and Gaza. More than 4,000 homes had been destroyed by the Israeli government since the Intifada began. Sharon and Abbas also met together in Egypt, where they announced an end to violence.

In August to September 2005, Prime Minister Sharon brought an end to Israeli occupation of Gaza. Although he was denounced by the Jewish settlers who had built their homes in Gaza, Sharon had obviously decided to try to begin a new era in Israeli-Palestinian relations. Many members of the Likud Party opposed Sharon. Therefore, the prime minister left Likud and formed a new party, called Kadima. Sharon believed that he could not negotiate with the Palestinians. Therefore, he was committed to establishing new borders for Israel on his own. He believed that small borders could be more easily defended. This involved withdrawing from Gaza and from more settlements on the West Bank. But Sharon's leadership was cut short when he suffered a massive stroke in January 2006.

The new leader of Kadima, Prime Minister Ehud Olmert, led his party to victory in elections in March 2006. He is committed to further Israeli withdrawal from the West Bank, which is supported by a majority of Israelis. Nevertheless, Olmert faces a new government in Palestine with a parliament controlled by Hamas, which won national elections in January. Hamas candidates defeated the members of Fatah, which had been the governing party. Many Palestinians were angry at Fatah, which they accused of corruption and of mismanaging the government. Although Abbas remained president of the Palestinian Authority, Hamas selected the new prime minister.

Hamas has long been committed to the destruction of Israel. Whether Olmert and the Hamas leaders can negotiate a new Israeli-Palestinian relationship or, if, instead, more violence will break out between the two sides is the major question looming for the future.

# Chronology

1000 BCE
King David establishes Jerusalem as Israel's capital

63 BCE
Israel, called Judea by the Romans, is made part of the
Roman Empire

132 CE
Jewish revolt stopped by Rome; Jews driven from Judea

570 CE
Birth of Muhammad

7th Century
Muslims conquer Middle East

1896
Theodor Herzl publishes *The Jewish State*; inspires First
Aliya, bringing immigrants to Palestine

1904
Second Aliya begins; more immigrants come to Palestine

1914–1918
World War I takes place

1917
Balfour Declaration issued

1919
Great Britain takes control of Palestine

1920
Violence flares in Palestine between Jews and Arabs

1929
Violence breaks out in Jerusalem

1936
Peel Report calls for partition of Palestine

1939–1945
World War II is fought

1947
United Nations calls for partition of Palestine

1948
Israel becomes a state; Palestinians become refugees

1949
Yasir Arafat founds Fatah

1954
War occurs in Suez Canal

1964
Palestinian Liberation Organization (PLO) founded

1967
Six Day War; Israel takes over West Bank and Gaza;
more Palestinians become refugees

1969
Arafat becomes head of PLO

1970
PLO driven from Jordan; moves headquarters to Lebanon

1973
Yom Kippur War takes place

1977
Egyptian President Anwar Sadat travels to Jerusalem
for peace talks

1978
Camp David meetings lead to Egyptian-Israeli peace
agreement

1981
Sadat assassinated

1982
Israel invades Lebanon and drives out the PLO

1987
Intifada breaks out

1990
Coalition led by United States defeats Iraq in the Persian
Gulf War

1991
Israel and Arab states meet in Madrid, Spain

1993–1995
Oslo Agreements lead to Palestinian territories

1995
Israeli Prime Minister Yitzhak Rabin assassinated by an Israeli

1998
Wye peace talks held in United States

2000
Peace talks break down at Camp David; another Intifada occurs

2001
Ariel Sharon elected prime minister of Israel

2001–2004
Palestinians begin suicide bombings; Israel attacks Palestinian settlements

2004
Yasir Arafat dies

2005
Mahmoud Abbas is elected president of the Palestinian Authority;
Israel withdraws from Gaza territories

2006
January
Hamas wins a majority in Palestinian parliament; Ariel Sharon
suffers massive stroke

March
Ehud Olmert elected prime minister of Israel

# Notes

Chapter 1

p. 7, par. 2, Greg Myre. "Israel Lowers Its Flag in the Gaza Strip," *The New York Times*, September 12, 2005.

p. 8, par. 3, Steven Erlanger. "Tearfully but Forcefully, Israel Removes Gaza Settlers," *The New York Times*, August 18, 2005.

p. 10, par. 1, Erlanger. "Israel Removes . . . ," *The New York Times*. August 18, 2005.

p. 11, par. 3, Arnold Blumberg. *The History of Israel*. Westport, CT: Greenwood Press, 1998, p. 69.

p. 11, par. 4, Cheryl Rubenberg. *The Palestinians: In Search of a Just Peace*. Boulder, CO: Lynne Rienner Publishers, 2003, p. 10.

p. 14, par. 1, William Dudley. *The Middle East: Opposing Viewpoints*, San Diego, CA: Greenhaven Press, 2004, p. 29.

p. 15, par. 1, Rubenberg, p. 135.

p. 15, par. 3, Barry Rubin, and Judith Culp Rubin. *Yasir Arafat: A Political Biography*. New York: Oxford University Press, 2003, p. 155.

p. 18, par. 2, James Kitfield. "Peace May Lie Only Beyond Sharon and Arafat," *National Journal*, April 13, 2002.

p. 18, par. 3, James Bennet. "Puzzle for Israel: What does Sharon Want," *The New York Times*, January 30, 2003.

p. 18, par. 4, Henry Siegman. "Sharon and the Future of Palestine," *The New York Review of Books,* December 2, 2004.

## Chapter 2

p. 22, par. 4–p. 23, pars. 1–3, Baruch Kimmerling, and Joel Migdal. *Palestinian People.* Cambridge, MA: Harvard University Press, 2003, pp. 34–35.

p. 28, par. 3, "Balfour Declaration, 1917," http://en.wikipedia.org/wiki/Balfour_Declaration_1917

p. 29, par. 2, "The Balfour Declaration," http://www.mideast web.org/mebalfour.htm

p. 29, par. 3, "Balfour Declaration," http://www.mideast web.org/mebalfour.htm

p. 30, par. 1, Jewish Virtual Library, Herbert Louis Samuel, http://www.jewishvirtuallibrary.org/jsource/biography/samuel.html

p. 31, par. 3, Jewish Virtual Library, "The Haganah," http://www.jewishvirtuallibrary.org/jsources/History/haganah.html

## Chapter 3

p. 39, par. 1, Baruch Kimmerling, and Joel Migdal. *Palestinian People,* Cambridge MA: Harvard University Press, 2003, pp. 152–153.

p. 40, par. 2–3, "Deir Yassin Massacre," http://en.wikipedia.org/wiki/Deir_Yassin_massacre

p. 40, par. 2, Ilan Pappe. *The Making of the Arab-Israeli Conflict, 1947–1951.* London: I. B. Tauris, 1994, p. 96.

p. 41, par. 3, Eric Silver. *Begin: The Haunted Prophet.* New York: Random House, 1984, p. 92.

p. 42, par. 1, Arnold Blumberg. *The History of Israel.* Westport, CT: Greenwood Press, 1998, p. 78.

p. 43, par. 3, "Deir Yassin Remembered," http://www.deiryassin.org/mams.html

p. 43, par. 4, Cheryl A. Rubenberg. *The Palestinians: In Search of a Just Peace.* Boulder, CO: Lynne Rienner Publishers, 2003, p. 11.

p. 44, par. 1, Kimmerling and Migdal, p. 159.

p. 44, par. 2, Kimmerling and Migdal, pp. 176–177.

p. 45, Sidebar. Roland Dallas. *King Hussein: A Life on the Edge.* New York: Fromm International, 1999, pp. 2, 3, 41.

p. 46, par. 3, "Gamal Abdul-Nasser," http://www.geocities.com/CapitolHill/Lobby/5270/bio.htm; "Famous Muslims: Gamal Abdul Nasser," http://www.famousmuslims.com/Gamal%20Abdul%20Nasser.htm

p. 48, par., 2, Chaim Herzog. *The Arab-Israeli Wars.* New York: Random House, 1982, p. 114.

p. 49, par., 2, Dallas, p. 98.

p. 50, par. 1, Dallas, p. 109.

p. 50, par. 2, Dallas, p. 112.

p. 50, par. 3, Herzog, pp. 149, 157.

p. 54, par. 1, David Hirst, and Irene Beeson. *Sadat,* New York: Faber and Faber, 1981, p. 98.

**Chapter 4**

p. 56, par. 2, Barry Rubin, and Judith Culp Rubin. *Yasir Arafat: A Political Biography.* New York: Oxford University Press, 2003, pp. 11–13.

p. 57, par. 1, Efraim Karsh. *Arafat's War.* New York: Grove Press, 2003, pp. 12–13.

p. 57, par. 2, Rubin and Culp Rubin, p. 20.

p. 58, par. 2, Rubin and Culp Rubin, p. 27.

p. 59, Sidebar. par. 1–3, Karsh, pp. 38–39.

p. 60, par. 2, Rubin and Culp Rubin, p. 35.

p. 61, par. 1, Dallas, pp. 130–132.

p. 62, par. 1, Rubin and Culp Rubin, p. 65.

p. 63, par. 2, Chaim Herzog. *Arab-Israeli Wars,* New York: Random House, 1982, p. 239.

p. 65, par. 1, Herzog, p. 288.

**Chapter 5**

p. 68, par. 3, Ahron Bregman, and Jihhan El-Tahri. *The Fifty Years' War*. New York: TV Books, 1999, p. 129.

p. 69, par. 1, David Hirst, and Irene Beeson. *Sadat*. New York: Faber and Faber, 1981, p. 174.

p. 70, par. 1, Hirst and Beeson, p. 186.

p. 70, par. 2, Roland Dallas. *King Hussein: A Life on the Edge*. New York: Fromm International, 1999, p. 157.

p. 70, par. 2, Hirst and Beeson, p. 190.

p. 70, par. 3, Blumberg, p. 124.

p. 70, par. 4, Hirst and Beeson, p. 195.

p. 71, par. 2, Jimmy Carter. *Keeping Faith: Memoirs of a President*. New York: Bantam Books, 1982, p. 273.

p. 72, par. 2, Anwar el-Sadat. *In Search of Identity*, New York: Harper and Row, 1978, p. 306.

p. 72, par. 4, Carter, p. 328.

p. 72, par. 5, Ahron Bregman, and Jihan El-Tahri. *The Fifty Years' War: Israel and the Arabs*. New York: TV Books, 1999, p. 153.

p. 73, par. 1, Eric Silver. *Begin*. New York: Random House, 1984, pp. 171–172.

p. 73, par. 2, Silver, p. 175.

p. 73, par. 3, Silver, pp. 175–176.

p. 73, par. 4, Bregman and El-Tahri, p. 157.

p. 74, par. 1, Silver, p. 179.

p. 74, par. 2, Silver, p. 191.

p. 74, par. 3, Carter, p. 351

p. 75, Sidebar, Bregman and El-Tahri, p. 165.

p. 76, par. 1, Carter, p. 356.

p. 76, par. 2, Silver, p. 197.

p. 76, par. 3, Silver, pp. 199–200.

**Chapter 6**

p. 79, par. 2, David Hirst, and Irene Beeson. *Sadat*. New York: Faber and Faber, 1981, p. 325.

p. 79, par. 3, Hirst and Beeson, p. 13.

p. 80, par. 2, Barry Rubin, and Judith Culp Rubin. *Yasir*

*Arafat: A Political Biography.* New York: Oxford University Press, 2003, p. 69.

p. 80, par. 3, Rubin and Culp Rubin, p. 80.

p. 82, par. 1, Arnold Blumberg. *The History of Israel.* Westport, CT: Greenwood Press, 1998, p. 144.

p. 82, par. 2, Ahron Bregman, and Jihan El-Tahri. *The Fifty Years' War,* New York: TV Books, 1999, p. 205.

p. 84, par. 1, Bregman and El-Tahri, p. 222.

p. 86, par. 3, Bregman and El-Tahri, p. 240.

p. 86, par. 4, Bregman and El-Tahri, p. 242.

p. 89, par. 1, Bregman and El-Tahri, pp. 306–307.

p. 91, par. 2, Rubin and Culp Rubin, pp. 150–152.

p. 91, pars. 2–3, Rubin and Culp Rubin, p. 153, 155.

p. 92, par. 1, Roland Dallas. *King Hussein: A Life on the Edge.* New York: Fromm International, 1999, p. 229.

p. 93, par. 1, Dallas, p. 279.

p. 93, par. 2, Efraim Karsh. *Arafat's War.* New York: Grove Press, 2003, p. 157.

p. 94, par. 3, Anton La Guardia. *War Without End: Israelis, Palestinians, and the Struggle for the Promised Land.* New York: St. Martin's Press, 2001, p. 268.

p. 95, pars. 1–2, Cheryl A. Rubenberg. *The Palestinians: In Search of a Just Peace.* Boulder, CO: Lynne Rienner Publishers, 2003, pp. 298, 300, 383.

p. 96, par. 1, Karsh, pp. 161, 162, 165.

p. 96, par. 2, La Guardia, p. 268.

Chapter 7

p. 98, par. 2, Cheryl A. Rubenberg. *The Palestinians: In Search of a Just Peace.* Boulder, CO: Lynne Rienner Publishers, 2003, p. 323.

p. 98, par. 3, Efraim Karsh. *Arafat's War.* New York: Grove Press, 2003, pp. 186–192.

p. 99, par. 1, Barry Rubin, and Judith Culp Rubin. *Yasir Arafat: A Political Biography.* New York: Oxford University Press, 2003, p. 206.

p. 99, par. 2, Rubenberg, p. 343.

p. 99, par. 3, "Israel Settlements and the Palestinian Uprising," *Economist*, April 28, 2001, p. 44.

p. 100, par. 1, Khalil Shikaki, "Palestinians Divided," *Foreign Affairs*, January/February, 2002.

p. 100, par. 2, Rubenberg, pp. 338–340.

p. 101, par. 2, Alexander Cockburn, "Sharon or Arafat: Which is the Sponsor of Terror," *Nation*, December 24, 2001.

p. 102, par. 2, David Remnick, "Checkpoint," *The New Yorker*, February 7, 2005.

p. 102, par. 3, Matt Rees, et al., "Fencing Off Terrorists," *Time*, June 17, 2002.

p. 103, par. 1, James Bennet, "Palestinians Fear Being Trapped by Israeli Wall," *The New York Times*, February 18, 2003.

p. 104, par. 2, Remnick.

p. 105, par. 1, Johanna McGeary, et al., "Road Map to Hell," *Time*, September 1, 2003.

p. 105, par. 3, Alexandre Trudeau, "Life on the Edge," *Maclean's*, May 3, 2004.

p. 106, par. 1, Remnick.

p. 106, par. 2, *Economist*, April 17, 2004.

p. 106, par. 3, "Sharon's Plan: A Shift from Occupation to Siege," *Washington Report on Middle East Affairs*, July/August, 2004.

# Further Information

## For Further Reading

Gunderson, Cory. *The Israeli-Palestinian Conflict.* Edina, MN: Abdo Publishers, 2004.

Hayhurst, Chris. *Israel's War of Independence.* New York: Rosen Publishing Group, 2004.

Holliday, Laurel, ed. *Children of Israel, Children of Palestine: Our Own True Stories.* New York: Pocket Books, 1998.

Marcovitz, Hal. *Jordan.* Philadelphia: Chelsea House, 2003.

Morrison, John. *Syria.* Philadelphia: Chelsea House, 2003.

Worth, Richard. *Ariel Sharon.* Philadelphia: Chelsea House, 2004.

## Web Sites

http://Nobelprize.org/peace/laureates

http://www.palestinefacts.org/pf_mandate_grand_mufti.php

http://www.spartacus.schoolnet.co.uk/PRsamuel.htm

# Bibliography

**Books**

Blumberg, Arnold. *The History of Israel.* Westport, CT: Greenwood Press, 1998.

Bregman, Ahron, and Jihan El-Tahri. *The Fifty Years' War: Israel and the Arabs.* New York: TV Books, 1999.

Carter, Jimmy. *Keeping Faith: Memoirs of a President.* New York: Bantam Books, 1982.

Dallas, Roland. *King Hussein: A Life on the Edge.* New York: Fromm International, 1999.

Dudley, William. *The Middle East: Opposing Viewpoints.* San Diego, CA: Greenhaven Press, 2004.

Hass, Amira. *Reporting from Ramallah.* Los Angeles: Semiotext(e), 2003.

Herzog, Chaim. *The Arab-Israeli Wars.* New York: Random House, 1982.

Hirst, David, and Irene Beeson. *Sadat.* New York: Faber and Faber, 1981.

Karsh, Efraim. *Arafat's War.* New York: Grove Press, 2003.

Kimmerling, Baruch, and Joel Migdal. *The Palestinian People.* Cambridge, MA: Harvard University Press, 2003.

La Guardia, Anton. *War Without End: Israelis, Palestinians, and the Struggle for a Promised Land*. New York: St. Martin's Press, 2001.

Remnick, David. "Checkpoint: A New Palestinian Leader Confronts Ariel Sharon," *The New Yorker*, February 7, 2005.

Rosenthal, Donna. *The Israelis*. New York: Free Press, 2003.

Rubenberg, Cheryl. *The Palestinians: In Search of a Just Peace*. Boulder, CO: Lynne Reinner, 2003.

Rubin, Barry, and Judith Culp Rubin. *Yasir Arafat: A Political Biography*. New York: Oxford University Press, 2003.

Shapiro, Samantha. "The Unsettlers," *The New York Times Magazine*, February 16, 2003.

Siegman, Henry. "Partners for War," *The New York Review of Books*, January 16, 2003.

Silver, Eric. *Begin: The Haunted Prophet*. New York: Random House, 2004.

Victor, Barbara. *Army of Roses: Inside the World of Palestinian Women Suicide Bombers*. New York: Rodale, 2003.

## Web Sites

http://www.famousmuslims.com

Jewish Virtual Library
http://www.jewishvirtuallibrary.org

MidEast Web-Documents and History
http://www.mideastweb.org/

Palestine Remembered
http://www.palestineremembered.com

Zionist Organization of America
http://www.zoa.org

# Index

Page numbers in **boldface** are illustrations.

**Richard Worth** is the author of more than fifty books. These include biographies, histories, and books on current events. Among his books are a biography of Ariel Sharon, a history of gunpowder, a biography of Nazi leader Heinrich Himmler, the award-winning *Gangs and Crime*, and a history of the slave trade. This is his first book for Marshall Cavendish Benchmark.